BAND ON THE RUN II: RUNNING ON EMPTY

BY

MATT SYVERSON

BACKSTAGE PASS PUBLISHING
VICTORIA, TX

All Rights Reserved. Copyright © 2012 Matt Syverson
No part of this book may be reproduced or transmitted in any form or by any means, graphic, electronic, or mechanical, including, but not limited to, photocopying, recording, taping or by any information storage or retrieval system, without the permission in writing from the author and publisher.

Names have been changed to protect the guilty.

For information, please contact:
Backstage Pass Publishing
P.O. Box 695
Victoria TX 77902
www.backstagepasspublishing.com

Author contact:
bowiefan1970@live.com

Cover Art by Tony Szatkowski.

Special thanks to my family, Mantis, and the readers of Black Dog and Band On The Run.

Printed by Lightning Source in the U.S. and U.K.
Also available as an ebook.

ISBN: 978-0-9854895-0-2

Dedicated to terriers everywhere

This is the sequel to 'Band On The Run'. If you haven't already read BOTR, you won't know what the hell is going on.

CHAPTER ONE

An idiot once said that life is like a box of chocolates – a box of chocolates that's been sitting in a hot car on a summer day, I say.

Sorry to start on such a negative slant, but I don't know what to say. It's been two years since I tried to write. If I wait for the perfect opening line, I'll never get anywhere.

CHAPTER TWO

Some first chapter, huh? You won't believe it, but that lousy start took me a month. My finger muscles were so atrophied from lack of use that I had to put a pencil in my mouth to type. I looked like one of those drinking bird toys from the seventies.

Don't worry – I've regained my strength enough to type in the normal manner.

***

You have questions, I know. You're wondering about that knock on my door the night Mellowtron signed their record contract.

Well, that was the hotel's concierge, not Sammy the Bull. He had a telegram for me from the old debutante I used to work for.

"James stop I'm dying stop teo torriate stop"

The old bitch still hadn't learned how to dial a telephone! (How did she know where I was, you ask? We kept in touch.)

As you know from the book that bastard, Matt Syverson, put out, I was in kind of a funk that night. It was way more than a funk, really. I was fully spun-out, 'Fear and Loathing in Las Vegas'-style, and the vodka I smuggled out of the party sure wasn't helping.

Overcome by emotion after receiving the message, I ran out of the room without a thought. I grabbed a backpack, but left my luggage and diary behind. I caught a bus, then a train, then a plane, and forty hours later I was in Tuscaloosa, Alabama, in the middle of the night, trying to catch a cab to Stringtown, Alabama.

An old black man in an unroadworthy vehicle finally picked me up.

"Get me to Stringtown, please!" I begged. I was worried I might arrive too late.

"You wants me ta takes ya alla way ta Stringtown? You crazy, mista!"

"I've got to get there as quickly as possible! Money is no object."

"Well..., thass a differnt story. Gimme a minute."

"Otis, come in Otis," the man spoke into the handset of a shiny new CB radio that stood out from the rest of the old vehicle's interior.

"This be Otis," came the reply through static.

"Waddup, cuz? Gots me a white boy here in Tha Loose who needs ta git ta S-Town. Meets me halfway?"

"A-ight," came the reply. Although only two syllables, the word was wrought with suspicion. "See y'all at the rest stop."

***

I was delivered to our meeting place on the side of the highway amid nonstop chatter from the driver. I was detached emotionally and gazed out into the stormy blackness, giving vague, "Um-hmms" and mumbling, "You got that right," when appropriate.

The rain was coming down in sheets as I exited the busted old taxi, only to climb into one that looked like it just came off the assembly line.

"Dry yo'self off, mista," the driver said, handing me a white hand towel. "Mind tha tuck and roll, please."

"Thank you, sir," I replied as I dried my face. "I didn't think they made cabs like this anymore. Where'd you get it?"

"Long story. My name's Otis. Relax, mista. Gon' be an hour and a half 'fore we gets ta Stringtown."

His soothing voice put me at ease, and I fell into a deep sleep without dreams. The trip had been stressful, full of stops and starts. I hadn't slept in days. As my eyes closed, I saw the driver look back at me in the rear-view mirror and smile. He had a gold front tooth.

I came to some time later after drifting in and out of consciousness in the spacious and semi-comfortable back seat of the taxi. I looked out the window and saw the sun was coming up. We were parked in front of an imposing old mansion, but it wasn't the debutante's house. The taxi driver was talking on his cell phone.

"Looks mighty nice, lil' bruva. You tell your boy Joe that everything been right as rain since y'all left. Okay? Okay. A'ight. Bye now and take care y'allselves."

"Where are we?" I asked after Otis hung up. I wanted to be cranky, but the old taxi driver was so nice it didn't take hold.

"We jus' outside Stringtown," he said. "Sorry 'bout the unplanned stop. Since we was up this way, and you was sleepin', I thought I'd check up on the house here for my lil' homeboys."

"It's not a problem," I said. "Do you know where the O'Day Mansion is?"

"Yessuh, course I do. Dat where y'all wants ta go?"

"Yes, please." I reclined and went back to sleep as the taxi pulled away from the curb. I didn't see a reason to stay awake. All I saw through the cab's window was a kudzu landscape.

***

A short time later we stopped, and the driver gave two quick bleats of the horn to wake me. I looked out and saw the long path leading up to the huge O'Day house I left years before.

"Why don't you drive on up?" I asked.

"The walk'll do you good, mista. And I can't take a

chance on gettin' stuck in tha mud or shot at. Tryin' ta keep my ride clean. It done rained the last two nights, too. Mosquitoes gon' be bad."

"Okay. What do I owe you, Otis?"

"Sixty-eight dollars, sir. Please tip generously, y'all."

He kept calling me y'all. I wondered why it was not obvious that I was traveling alone, but gave the cab driver eighty bucks and got out.

I started out on the two-hundred-yard path to the old mansion, somewhat hesitant to end my journey. I had been away from the South long enough that I had mentally estimated the distance in yards – I should have thought two football fields. In the South, distance is nearly always measured in football fields.

The little road had two deep grooves made by vehicular travel years ago, but was now being reclaimed by thick grass tendrils and tentacles of kudzu.

It had been three years since I had seen the old dame, and I dreaded witnessing her on her deathbed. I don't mean I regretted coming to visit her. I was concerned as to how she would appear after a prolonged illness. She looked worse than Skeletor on her best days when she employed me.

Hundred-year-old oak trees lined both sides of the path as I walked down the lane, their canopies meeting overhead. The temperature wasn't high, but the humidity was overwhelming. Sweat poured from my forehead. A thumb-sized bug buzzed by me like a helicopter attempting an emergency landing. It made a vibrating, rattling racket – a locust. Responses rose from every tree at an ear-splitting volume. Mosquitoes swarmed me. I became confused and disoriented and broke into a sprint toward the antebellum mansion.

I reached the enormous columned porch and ascended

the concrete steps two at a time. I stumbled to the huge doors and lifted my hand to knock. I saw the quick flash of an eyeball through the peep-hole just before the door flew open. The knuckles of my right hand rapped three times on the forehead of a young Hispanic guy. It all happened very quickly.

"¿Porque? ¡No bueno!" The under-sized, brown-skinned man grabbed his forehead with both hands and gave me a hateful look.

I reached into my backpack to find my pocket translator. I tapped at the keypad as the Hispanic guy struck a karate pose, preparing to defend himself. "Jag är ledsen," I muttered, not looking up from the electronic device.

"I not Swedish, Yames. You hit wrong button. I do accept the apology of you." He had an unplaceable Latin-American accent. He dropped his lethal weapons and extended a handshake.

I was shaken. For the first time in my life, I had met someone possibly more sophisticated and suave than me. I crumpled into a fetal pile.

***

I woke some time later in a four-post canopy bed. I was so exhausted from my trip that I had slept thirty hours, although I was not aware of it. I immediately recognized that I was in the 'Canine' bedroom, one of at least a dozen in the old house, each categorized by a nickname inspired by the decorating theme. Antique dog figurines accessorized every available horizontal plane. I rolled over and saw a fist-sized sculpture of a Boston Terrier with an underbite glaring at me from the shelved headboard.

"Ruff, ruff!" a voice barked, shocking me like a lightning bolt down a kite string.

I twisted involuntarily toward the sound and saw the

Hispanic man approaching me with a tray of breakfast goodies. I noticed he had a set of buck-teeth that would have made a teenage Freddie Mercury regain his self-esteem.

"Scared, no?" he said, trying to stifle his smile. "You eat now. Welcome home, Mr. Yames."

I felt like James Bond. Wasn't he always a guest of some evil genius – treated like royalty by someone trying to kill him?

"What's going on?" I demanded. "Who are you, and where is she?"

The man set the tray on a side table. I glared at him. *Is this man my adversary?* I asked myself, once again thinking of the Ian Fleming novels I had devoured as a young man. He *did* look like one of the bad guys from a Bond movie – short, foreign, bald, and buck-toothed. He was the exact opposite of Bond's arch-enemy, Jaws, actually.

"Me name Roberto," he said, extending his hand in a slightly fey manner. I lightly grasped and shook his paw. I deduced I was in no danger as I compared his handshake to prior ones, like Nicky Pepperonzi's. He reached for the tray and held it out in front of me. "The legs, Mr. Yames?"

I was confused for an instant, then folded the legs down from the tray, so it straddled me when he set it down. I snaked backward and sat up against the headboard without disturbing the steaming coffee suspended inches above my crotch.

"Where's the old debutante?" I said as I cut off a corner of French toast. I'll admit I was being a bit gruff, but it was something I had picked up from Nicky on the road. I still hadn't decompressed.

Roberto motioned with his arms as he spoke, hoping it would help me interpret his sentence fragments. "Woman go away now. She travel to happy hunting ground." He made more extravagant motions in sign-language meant to aid my understanding.

"She's dead?!"

"Yes, so sorry I am. She is burned the day you get here."

"Burned?!" I was confused. Just waking from a two-day nap wasn't helping. I was beyond groggy.

"She there is," Roberto said, pointing to a small teal-colored vase sitting on a little antique table in front of the window.

"Leave me now!" I ordered. Before the last word of my command slithered across my chapped lips, Roberto was gone. For the first time in years, I felt utterly alone.

I moved the tray and folded back the old quilts covering me and stepped onto the oak hardwood floor. I looked down and saw that I was swaddled in a primitive cotton cloth wrapping of some sort, no doubt installed by Roberto. I imagined myself in a dying cockroach pose being diapered by the lad and shuddered like a dog after a bath.

I stepped over to the vase and picked it up. It was tiny. I took the nipple-ish apex of the lid between two fingers, removed it, and looked inside. I was perplexed. I saw no ashes. I turned the vase upside down over my left palm, and a pellet the size of a children's chewable aspirin dropped into my hand.

Holy crap, I thought. She must have wasted away to nothing! Keith Richards said he snorted a line of his father's ashes. This little nugget wouldn't even make a decent bump. I thought for a second of smoking it in a pipe, but realized I wasn't trying to out-Keef Keith Richards, after all. I put the bitter pill back in the ceramic vessel, capped it, and put it on a shelf next to a three-inch-tall Westie figurine.

What now? I had come all this way, had completely blown off the band, the tour, everything. I brought my hands to my face and withered, falling onto the bed and bouncing the tray and my breakfast to the floor.

"Oh, let me to get that, Mr. Yames," Roberto said as he swooped in. Had he been in the room the whole time?

I wailed and wailed in hysterical, convulsing sobs.

"There, there, Mr. Yames," Roberto soothed. I felt him stick his finger into the waist of my loin-wrap and tug to peer in and determine if I was due for a change.

"WAAAAHHH," I howled, humiliated on top of my pain. I was further heartbroken that I hadn't been able to place the old loofah in the debutante's coffin at her viewing.

And thus began my exile.

CHAPTER THREE

Two years passed, in which I did virtually nothing but mourn, incapacitated. I started out mourning the old dame, but that eventually morphed into mourning my life, the band, and everything else I had lost.

I was catatonic. I spent my days staring out the window or sitting on the porch with a glazed expression, not lifting a finger. As I stated, my muscles withered to the point that I could not manage to walk up or down the stairs, just like the old debutante. Faced with the same scenario decades earlier, she had installed a stair lift – a mechanical device that raises a chair up or down the stairs while the invalid sits in it. Henry VIII had a similar machine that employed a bevy of servants and a block and tackle system, but this one simply had a hidden chain powered electrically with a car battery back-up, not much different than a garage door opener.

The only downside to the stair lift was that the stairs were numerous, and the device was slow. It took nearly ten minutes for a one-way trip. Thankfully, my trusty servant, Roberto, aka 'Robo', was always available to retrieve any article I had forgotten from above or below. Sometimes he even threw me over his shoulder and hauled me up or down the stairs if he was going the same way as me.

I can't tell you how much my little Robo helped me through this period, although those with knowledge of depression or addiction might say he was 'enabling' me. Whatever you want to call it, I'll just say that the duties he performed for me were virtually the same as those of the debutante he worked for previously, my old bitch.

Robo and I were inseparable, other than when he ran errands with Otis, the cab driver. He was like my ever-present little beaver-toothed shadow. I never had to tell him my drink was empty or that I was ready to be wiped – he always knew. I don't think I ever gave him a command after saying "Leave me now!" when I found out the old debutante had died and been cremated without me.

Over the course of the two years in my self-imposed exile, I never once watched TV, read a book or magazine, or listened to the radio. I just existed, withering away like a bouquet of dead flowers. My mind deteriorated along with my muscles until I was almost a vegetable – not far above the zucchini on the evolutionary ladder. Not having to verbally command Robo regarding my needs, I became almost speechless. The only phrase I regularly used was, "I'll have my eggs poached for breakfast, I guess."

It goes without saying that the life of a shut-in is rather boring. The sight of a sparrow passing my window would bring me to spastic clapping and retarded laughter.

One day I was napping on a sultry afternoon. Due to the size of the house, air conditioning was rarely used. Thus, ceiling fans were employed to battle the heat and humidity, sometimes two in one room. I woke from my sleep in the 'Jesus' bedroom with two sets of blades whirling above me. I was drenched in sweat and surrounded by pictures and icons of the Man, Himself. Mentally emaciated, I struggled to remember who this long-haired dude all around me was. Maybe he was a rock star. He seemed nice, so I smiled like a happy idiot. I looked out the window and was blinded by the Alabama sun. I felt for the two-way intercom speaker on the nightstand, unable to see anything but white.

I pushed the button two times – two clicks – a signal Robo would recognize, so I would not have to speak.

Robo pressed 'TALK' and promptly answered from the kitchen. "Are your napping done, mister Yames? I wrist deep in pollo enchiyadas, but I be there soon as hoomanly possible! Is okay?"

My expression was frozen, as if my face had been clear-coated with ceramic glaze and fired in a kiln. I had heard familiar music playing behind Robo's words. I pressed the 'LISTEN' button, so I could hear the sounds of the kitchen. Robo was cooking and singing along to a song on the radio.

"*Mick's lips, Mick's lips, what if my lips were as big as Mick's, three feet wide and four feet thick...*"

I smiled stupidly and attempted to focus on a large portrait of the Savior. My sight came back slowly, and good old J.C. materialized before me like a spiritual vision. From somewhere deep inside, a thought of Jedediah Kanobi drifted into my vacant skull. I closed my eyes and moved my head back and forth like a mentally challenged Stevie Wonder. A spontaneous daydream of Cal E. Fornia performing an exquisite scissor-kick in orange, nut-hugging spandex tights flashed in my mind. I threw my head back and laughed, semi-coherent for the first time in ages.

Robo charged into the room, thinking something was amiss.

"Mister Yames, Mister Yames, what is the wrong? Are you having the stroke again?!"

"Owwooooo!!!" I yelled, my lungs fully expanding for the first time since I arrived at the O'Day house. "I'm gonna find the band, Robo! Those bastards can't do it without me!" The words strained my vocal chords, and I burst into dry coughing.

Robo was in tears, terrified. "Mister Yames, what about is this? No bueno!"

"No bueno? Muy bueno, you beautiful moron!" I choked, tears in my eyes. I was ecstatic – on the verge of speaking in one of the lost tongues of jive. "Muy, muy bueno! I'm alive, Robo! Alive, I tell you! Let the midnight special shine its ever-lovin' light on me!"

I lurched to my feet and jumped as high as I could – six epic inches – shocking what muscles I had left. I fell to the floor and flopped like a trout, seizuring.

Robo dropped his weight on me and stuck his fingers down my throat to keep me from swallowing my tongue, which I would have preferred.

"No bueno, no bueno," he repeated softly in my ear as he cradled me and rocked back and forth, his hand still deep in my mouth.

***

Perhaps this had all come on a bit fast – it took two weeks for me to recover from the excitement. Robo rarely left my bedside, spooning homemade menudo into my pie-hole tirelessly. Being somewhat 'backwards', for lack of a more politically correct term, Robo thought I had been possessed by an evil spirit. He insisted on praying over me in a language I could not recognize, but the prayer sessions actually made me feel better. I needed all the help I could get. He performed rituals, applied poultices, and rubbed my chest and forehead with all sorts of ancient remedies. Surprisingly, I felt strengthened after each procedure.

During my recovery, I told Robo what I could remember of my back-story. He knew virtually nothing about me, but had been my closest friend of late, so I opened up to him. This was a strange dynamic, like the Lone Ranger telling Tonto his darkest secrets from a time before they met.

Robo was the perfect listener, thanks to his time with the old debutante. I spilled my guts. Over and over again, though, my eyes were drawn to his enormous choppers, which caused me to lose my train of thought. I felt bad, since I noticed Robo's lips straining to hide his domino-sized teeth each time. At some point, I hoped the boy would be able to grow a large mustache to act as a curtain over his mouth, but as for now, Robo was as hairless as a light bulb.

Robo never once tried to counsel me, which was right. I needed to talk it out and come to terms with myself – with my substance abuse, with my power-tripping, with my problems with authority.

One day Robo came into my room and tossed a book onto the bed next to me. I picked it up – 'Personality Plus'. I glanced at Robo, and he returned a Freudian look. Or maybe it was Jungian.

"It from the library is, Mr. Yames. Take a read. See you at the dinner, Mr. Yames."

I picked up the little paperback and opened it, curious. It was a self-help type book, but it turned out to be interesting. It told how to determine your personality type, as well as those of others, so you can understand your behavior and learn how other people perceive you. The book clarified the motivations behind people's actions – what makes them tick, in other words.

By the time Robo entered the room with a large bowl of hearty soup for me that evening, I had finished most of the book.

"Robo, this book has helped me so much!"

"Yes, Mr. Yames. Eat before the food cold is."

Knowing I wanted to finish, Robo fed me as I read the final chapter.

Finally, I closed the paperback and set it by my shriveled left leg. Using a term from the book, Robo said, "You too choleric, Mr. Yames. You can't give away the control."

"Robo, you're a genius. I see. For the first time, I can really see."

"Cal sanguine is. He a peacock."

"Always the life of the party," I said. "And Domino is phlegmatic – he doesn't have an opinion. He's easily influenced. Headley is melancholy, because he's an artist."

"Sponge a dope fiend is," Robo said. We both laughed.

"Robo, you're a good guy."

"Oh, Mister Yames, you a good guy, too. I must need to clean up after the dinner." He picked up the tray with the empty bowl and made his way out the door into the hall.

"Robo," I called softly.

"Yes, Mister Yames," he said as he re-appeared in the doorway.

"That was the best soup I've ever eaten. I do believe it has restored something in me. What do you call it?"

"Loofah soup."

My eyes were frozen planets as a dry arctic wind swept across a woolly mammoth graveyard in the tundra of my mind.

"You are welcome, Mr. Yames," Robo said as he walked away.

***

I spent the rest of the night scribbling in a notebook – drawing charts and Venn diagrams, even diagramming sentences I had spoken in the past. I realized how dysfunctionally I had managed Mellowtron. I drew them close at times, only to lash out at them in a rage a short time later.

For the first time since rushing out of the Drake Hotel, I thought of Crisco and his happy dog grin. God, I missed that greasy mutt! I burst into tears and thrust myself onto my bed and sobbed until I fell asleep.

***

Next thing I knew, I was sitting in a chair on the screened-in back porch of an old mansion unfamiliar to me.

It was the middle of the night. A violent howl broke the silence as I tried to adjust my eyes to the darkness.

"What be dat?" an old black man sitting to the left of me asked. He was slender, dressed in a tailored suit and wearing a dapper hat cocked at an extreme angle. A hand-rolled cigarette drooped from his mouth, and a vintage steel-string acoustic guitar rested against the arm of the wicker chair in which he sat.

"I don't know, mister," I said, trying to place myself. I looked around and saw I was sitting among a loosely assembled group of people relaxing on the rest of the porch's furniture.

"Behold the ancient night, Robert Johnson," came a crooning voice to my right. I turned to see a slightly bloated white guy in brown leather pants and a pirate shirt. He had a full beard and wavy hair and continually drifted into different poses, as if someone was taking his picture for the cover of Rolling Stone.

"Jim, do you always gotta talk like a poym?" rasped a Southern Comfort-scarred voice, female but not feminine. The woman sat on the far side of the couch next to Jim. Her face was plain-Jane, without make-up, but she had feathers in her hair and wore a ton of costume jewelry. "Sounded like a dang werewolf or a chupacabra. Done scared me!" She had a disarming Texas accent and a kind face.

"Now, Janis," Jim said back to her. "There's no such thing as either of those. It was probably just a twentieth-century fox."

"Dang-it, Jim," the happy-go-lucky broad said with a cackle. "You're always quotin' your crazy lyrics. How 'bout you show me the way to the next whiskey bar?" She threw an arm over his shoulders and pulled him close to her. They were obviously old friends.

"Oh, moon of Alabama," Jim sang flatly with his head down – too lazy or drunk to care if he was on key. Then, as if plugged in, his body spasmed and he raised his head and howled, "OWWUUOOOUUAAAAH!!" His ragged voice covered multiple octaves and ended in a primal scream.

"You're crazy, the bleedin' lot a ya!" declared an angry voice with a Camden accent. "You wankers are driving me bloody batty! Makes we wanna bloomin' honk."

The words came from a skinny chick seated in a chair next to the couch Jim and Janis sat on. She was barely five-feet-tall, but wore her hair in an enormous black beehive. Her teeth looked like the aftermath of a pile-up on the Autobahn. I glanced down at her blood stained, satin ballet slippers. She gave me a dirty look and gestured at me with two fingers. I had no idea who she was.

"Ignore her, James," Janis said. "She's new, and she ain't come to terms. Her name's Wino."

"It ain't!" the British bird chirped.

I was beginning to have some idea of what was going on, since I recognized most of the faces in the group. "How old are all of you?" I asked.

"We're twenty-seven, James," a grungy looking dude with dirty-blonde hair said from behind me. "Hope I die before I get old, right?"

"How old *you* be, mista?" the old blues man asked me as he picked up his guitar. I noticed that I saw him in black and white, while the others were in color. "You done reached tha crossroads of yo' life, son."

"I'm twenty-seven, too," I said. "Am I dead?"

"You are very much alive, mate, though we are not," a soft Cockney voice said. "We all suffered death by misadventure, but you've still got a punter's chance, James. You're only dreaming."

I turned to face the speaker, a man with a bowl haircut of thick blonde locks and the puffiest eyes I'd ever seen. He was sitting on the floor with his legs crossed in front of him like an Indian Swami.

"You're..., you're," I mumbled.

"Brian Jones of my Rolling Stones."

"Oh my God."

"Lucky you don't have a swimming pool, James. You would have checked out ages ago. There's still time for you, mate. Did you know Bobby Dylan bought the casket I was buried in? And did you see the boys' concert for me at Hyde Park?"

"I saw pictures," I said. "It was nice. Mick read a poem – Byron, I think."

"Percy Shelley, actually," Brian Jones replied. "As much as I'd like to reminisce, we're getting off topic, James. The 27 Forever Club is here for a reason."

"James, you didn't appreciate what you had with your band," Cobain said. "I didn't either."

"You're right, Kurt. Everything I worked for is gone," I said, on the verge of tears. "I fear it's too late to get back."

"Castles made of sand melt into the sea, eventually," answered a familiar voice. I felt a gentle hand touch my shoulder. I turned my head slowly to see who it was, though I had a strong suspicion who I would see. Jimi Hendrix stood over me with a kind smile on his face. You can fill in the description beyond that – he looked exactly like you imagine.

At this point, I was overwhelmed – questioning reality as in all the best dreams.

"James, you gotta do what you can before it's too late. You're only gonna live one time," Janis said. She seemed genuinely concerned. "You gotta get it while ya can. I'd trade all of my tomorrows for one single yesterday."

Brian Jones spoke next. "Time is on your side, but not for long, James."

"You're the one who's got to die when it's your time to go," Jimi said. "Don't forget that."

Someone rapped on the screen door of the porch, scaring all of us.

"Hey guys!"

I looked at the person at the door, shocked. It was Chris Farley, smiling broadly, his unkempt hair jutting in all directions.

"Tommy-boy!" I said before I could stop myself. A heavy-set man with a stubbly beard stood beside him – John Belushi. This was the most amazing dream I had ever had.

"We're lookin' for the 33 Forever Comedians meeting," Belushi said. "We're lost." He arched one eyebrow and glared at his friend.

"Sorry, man," Farley said. "I'm such a screw-up!" He slapped his hand hard against his own forehead.

"I tried to tell you we were lost," Belushi said. "BUT NOOO, did you listen?!" Farley looked back at him like a scolded pet, tears welling in his puppy-dog eyes.

"I'M A MORON!!" he wailed.

"It's okay, baby," soothed Janis. "Don't beat yourself up so bad."

"The purpose of a journey is not to arrive," Morrison said, staring intensely into Farley's eyes. "You should be happy to be lost. That's when you'll find what you're looking for." Farley looked scared and somewhat hypnotized.

"John, I think I remember the way now," Farley muttered, still glued to Morrison's eyes. "Let's get the hell outta here."

Belushi looked at me and shrugged his shoulders with a

'watcha gonna do?' expression. The two tragic comedians turned and walked away into the dense fog. Belushi put his hand on Farley's thick shoulder as they disappeared, counseling his protégé.

"Dog's bollocks!" the beehived chick yelled, startling the rest of us. "Can we please bugger off?"

"We gots ta go, son," Robert Johnson said in a kind voice. "You gon' be okay, James." He stood up and opened the screen door to leave.

"Please stay longer," I said, standing up.

"I'm coming too, Mr. Johnson," Brian Jones called out as he rushed past me after the old man. "Be a darling and show me that chord again."

"James, you'll know what to do," Janis said to me as she stood up to leave. "Follow your heart, honey." She smiled at me, then paused to look back toward the couch. "C'mon, Jim!" she yelled at Morrison, who had fallen asleep. "We're fixin' to go, sweetie!" She kicked him in the shin lightly and rushed off like she was worried about being left behind.

Morrison snorted and woke, out of it.

"I need to know more!" I pleaded.

Morrison rose and staggered up to me. He put his hand on my shoulder and jutted his face forward until it was inches from my own. He cocked his head dramatically and said, "This is the end, my confused friend."

I stood, dumbfounded, as he slammed his forearms against the rickety screen door and stumbled away.

"Don't do drugs, James," Cobain said as he followed the others. He opened the door gently and shut it softly behind him before walking off.

The dead musicians grouped at the edge of the backyard, then walked into the foggy forest together.

"Finally rid of 'em!" the skinny chick said to me.

"Bloody tossers."

I glared at her, not attempting to mask my irritation.

She looked back at me and leaned back in her chair and looked away.

"You're not staying here," I said.

She whipped her face toward me with a hateful sneer, but got up quickly and left. "Wankers, the lot of ya," she complained as she slammed the screen door behind her. "Where can a bird get a bloody kebab around here?" she asked rhetorically as she walked off in the direction the others had gone.

I stared into the night, now quiet as crystal, for many moments, thinking.

Finally, I turned and walked to the door of the house and opened it and went inside.

CHAPTER FOUR

I woke the next morning, feeling like I had died and been resurrected. Robo skipped in and sat down on the bed next to me.

"Morning, Mr. Yames! Did you have the good sleep?"

"Good question, Robo. I don't really know. I had a very interesting dream."

"Do you need to me to talk, Mr. Yames? I will get your breakfast and to me you will talk."

"I'll be coming down to the kitchen for breakfast today, Mr. Robo."

Robo looked back at me with his mouth agape, then smiled.

"Mr. Yames, you want me to carry Mr. Yames?" He curtsied slightly like a unicorn allowing herself to be mounted.

"That won't be necessary, Robo. And I won't be taking the stair-lift, either."

Robo wiggled all over like an excited puppy. "Mr. Yames, I so proud!"

"Thanks, buddy. It may take a while, so you go on ahead and prepare breakfast. I'll see you as soon as hoomanly possible."

"Oh, Mr. Yames, you are always making the fun!"

He rushed out, elated, leaving me alone with the task before me. I might as well have said I was going to run the Boston Marathon.

"What have you gotten yourself into, James?" I said aloud. "Here goes nothing."

I threw the covers back and got out of bed achingly slow. I took small steps toward the door as if I was shackled in leg irons. I reached the hall and sighed at the length of it.

Realizing it would be lunch time when I got to the kitchen at the rate I was managing, I attempted to go faster.

My tendons and ligaments had drawn up like the sinewy fat in an old piece of beef jerky. My knees were virtually petrified. I stumbled forward like a rusty Tin Man, taking choppy steps. It felt as if I had two-by-fours lashed to my legs, so I swiveled my hips and swung them forward like C-3PO re-learning to walk at a physical therapy session for disabled droids. *James, you have really let yourself go*, I thought.

I reached the top of the stairs and wanted desperately to sit in the comfortable stair-lift chair and drift down like a snowflake, but did not. It took some time for me to determine a strategy for descending. I wasn't agile enough to safely step down, so I weighed the pros and cons of head-first or foot-first.

I decided that the safest method would be to proceed head-first on my belly, letting gravity do most of the work. I would place my hands on each step in front of me while my body slid down slowly – basically just trying not to lose control.

I started down in this manner, but by the third step my arms felt like overcooked fettuccine. Unable to stop my momentum, my body slid forward – the friction against the carpet my only ally against evil gravity. I coasted to a stop on the landing, halfway down the stairs. The front of my body was now a carpet burn – my soft white underbelly was red and inflamed.

Robo appeared at the bottom of the steps and watched me examine my injuries.

"Mr. Yames, please let me to carry you."

"No, Robo. I've got to do this myself. Bring me a pillow – the largest you can find."

Robo ran off, but quickly returned and ascended the steps carrying a giant velour pillow – the equivalent of a bean bag.

"This was to her the favorite," Robo said as he set the pillow on the landing.

"Hot pink, of course," I replied.

We both thought of the old debutante and grew emotional. I reached out and hugged my little friend.

"Why you want to be strong again, Mr. Yames?" Robo asked, tears filling his dark eyes.

"My life has been on hold for long enough, Robo. I've got work to do."

I sat down on the back end of the pillow and motioned to Robo. "Get on. The train is leaving the station."

"All the people must get on the board," he said, trying to shake off his sadness.

"You're supposed to say 'all aboard', Robo."

He smiled and sat down in front of me, and I held his sides firmly.

"Now we go, Mr. Yames!" Robo put his left hand on the wall and his right on a stair spindle and pushed.

We sailed down the twenty or so stairs and crash landed, tumbling nearly to the front door.

"Mr. Yames, are you okay?" Robo said, laughing.

"What's for breakfast, you little idiot? I'm starving."

***

I picked up a shard of crispy bacon and bit off a healthy piece, which triggered a muscle memory that triggered a mental memory of driving the Sopwith Camel and munching on Bohemian garlic beef jerky from a smokehouse in Texas. Recollections were coming back quick and often. My mental capacity was recharging.

"Robo, you've been my best friend and loyal

manservant the last two years. That's something special, and I appreciate it."

"Yes, Mr. Yames. I'm the best friend."

"Don't get cocky, Bugs," I said. A jolt of nauseating guilt shot through me. Since reading the book about personalities, I was noticing when I was being a dick, and it was making me almost physically ill. It was kind of like Alex from 'A Clockwork Orange' after his aversion therapy. And I was feeling some foreign emotion – remorse? Whatever it was, it was new to me.

"Sorry 'bout that," I said.

"Sorry for the what?"

Apparently, Robo didn't know about Bugs Bunny and rabbit teeth and hadn't gotten the mean joke. I felt stupid for apologizing.

"Oh, nothing, Robo. Nothing. Where was I?"

"To you I am the number one," Robo said.

"Yes, that's exactly right. You're my best friend, little buddy."

I paused to eat some of the migas Robo had prepared. It was very good. "This migas is very good, Robo."

"Thanks to you, Mister Yames."

I couldn't hold my tongue any longer. "I've got a favor to ask you, and you can say no, Robo. I'd do it myself if I could, but I'm just not up to it. I need more time to recuperate. I've been vegging out for a while now, you know." I was rambling.

"On me you can count, Mr. Yames. Tell to me what the thing it is."

"I'm just not strong enough yet, Robo. Look at me! I've got the body of an eighty-year-old man."

"Tell to me what is the thing to do I must!" he begged, eager to please me.

"You've got to go out there!" I said, thrusting my index finger in the direction of the kitchen window and the world outside. "You've got to find everybody I've told you about and bring them here, Robo!" I slammed the table hard with my fist, rattling the dishes and sending a tremor of pain up my fragile arm. I didn't know it, but I had given myself numerous stress fractures. "Goddamn it, I can't do it myself!" I slumped in my chair, tears streaming down my cheeks.

"I will do for you this, Mr. Yames," Robo said with determination, staring out the window with a concrete gaze. He looked like he was posing for the fifth spot on Mount Rushmore. "I will go forward to these people and tell to them your story!"

***

We decided that Robo would embark three days later at precisely 7:00 a.m. The day was still young, and there were many things to do, so I raced up the stairs to make a list of things I would need while Robo was gone. (Okay, I walked up the first three steps, then Robo carried me the rest of the way. I can't seem to tell a lie since I read that damn personality book!)

I sat on my bed and attempted to document what I would need when left to myself. I imagined walking up and down the aisles at Wal-Mart and plucking things from the shelves and wrote down each item. I realized there wasn't much I *didn't* need. I started in the drug and beauty part of the store, and it went something like this – aspirin, yes, ibuprofen, yes, allergy pills, yes, Nyquil, yes, lotion, yes, cotton balls, yes, Q-tips, yes, shampoo, yes, conditioner, yes, eye drops, yes, tweezers, yes, fingernail clippers, yes, toenail clippers, yes, and so on.

I became so preoccupied with my health and beauty needs that I didn't bother to document the food and drink I would need – but I had faith that Robo could be trusted with this. Little did I know that my little Robo was downstairs at that very moment, taking inventory of the pantry and planning nourishing meals and special treats for me in his absence.

Later, I met Robo at the landing of the stairs for a picnic lunch, and yes, I made it there on my own.

"Robo, what's up with the money? Where's it been coming from?" I asked. I had never before considered who or what had funded the last two years of my pitiful existence, but the lights and water had remained on. There was a source of income somewhere, and I was determined to find it.

"The money letters come on the third of the days of the month," Robo replied.

"Are you saying a check comes every month?"

"On the third of the days of the month comes the one special check."

"And you cash it?"

"I sign the name of the woman, just as always I have done."

I was speechless, my mind racing. Robo was committing Social Security fraud without knowing it!

"Do you have the envelopes from those letters, Robo?"

"I have a bag filled with many letters."

"Get them!" I demanded.

Robo set his olive loaf sandwich down on his paper plate and bounded down the stairs into an infrequently used room.

He returned with an old duffel bag that looked to be Civil War-era. He unzipped it and dumped its ample contents onto the landing in front of me. Unopened envelopes spilled down the stairs. I recognized similarities and began separating the correspondence into piles. Some were full-sized envelopes, addressed by hand. Some looked like computer-generated government correspondence with clear plastic address windows. Others were manila envelopes with the return address of law firms.

"Show me what kind of letter has been delivering the checks you signed, Robo. Is it like any of these?"

"The most recent one in the kitchen is, Mr. Yames. I have not taken it to a bank."

"Well...?" I said.

Robo hopped up and raced downstairs and returned with the envelope. He handed it to me, and I saw it wasn't like the others. It was an 11x17 inch manila. The return address was that of an accounting firm in Auburn.

I glanced at Robo skeptically, and he diverted his eyes as if he was guilty of something.

I opened the envelope and pulled out a thick set of papers.

I tried to make sense of the figures on the first page, but I was no accountant. I scanned through page one, then through two, three, four, and so on. I was googly-eyed from all the zeros, but it was all summed up nicely at the bottom of the fifteenth page.

"*Accumulated revenue across all accounts, including losses for the month, equals $20,405.68.*"

The sixteenth page of correspondence had a check for that very amount.

"Oh, my God, Robo! What have you been doing with all this money?"

"Nothing, Mr. Yames! I to me have only received my pay of the two-hundred dollars for each week. Did I do wrong?!"

"Are you saying you only make $800 a month, Robo?"

"Yes, Mr. Yames. Is too much? Do you want my money

to be returned?"

"Of course not. You're worth much more than that. You said you signed the checks, though, Robo. What happened to the rest of the money?"

"It is in the deposit."

"It was deposited?"

"Yes, Mr. Yames. I am not the one who will steal. I shall not!"

I exhaled, relieved. "Thank God, Robo. I thought we were going to have to money launder you."

Robo blew out a breath, imitating me. He had no idea what was going on.

We were still sitting on the landing of the stairs. This was no place for a business meeting of this magnitude.

"Robo, gather up these envelopes and meet me in the formal dining room." I picked up my pillow and sat on it and pushed off down the stairs.

Fifteen minutes later we had separated all the different types of envelopes and stacked them in neat piles in front of their own seat at the dining table, which was enormous. It could easily accommodate twenty people, so there were a number of empty place settings.

"Okay, Robo," I said. "We need to organize each stack from oldest to newest, back to front. I want the envelope facing the chair to be the latest statement."

Robo and I worked for another half hour. It was now well past lunch, so we took a break to enjoy an afternoon treat of homemade empenadas. We sat at the glossy walnut table and smiled at each other as we snacked.

I ate methodically, chewing each bite dozens of times. I had little idea of what the envelopes in front of me contained, but my mind was racing, knowing Robo's little fingers had long ago memorized and perfected the strokes of the old dame's signature. I was mentally justifying a large severance package for both of us.

Finally, I could wait no longer. I swallowed the last bite of my empenada and opened the front envelope of the pile nearest to me. I nodded with my lips pursed tightly, then continued down the table. My hands shook as I opened the next, then the next. By the time I held the last envelope in my hand, I was sweating and gritting my teeth – essentially tweaking as I tried to comprehend the figures dancing on the pages between commas and decimal points.

Robo sat and watched silently. He was sure he had done something dreadfully wrong. I had made my way completely around the table before either of us said a word.

"Mr. Yames, did I breaking the law?"

"Robo, do you know what 'power of attorney' means? Have you ever heard that before?"

"Yes, I am the power of a attorney."

"How many people came to the old lady's funeral, Robo?"

"Yust me and Mr. Yames, but you did not to make it, Mr. Yames."

"Excellent."

***

Any sense of urgency I had about Robo leaving was now lifted. I informed him that his departure was postponed indefinitely, so as not to rush our preparations. Robo was relieved, since he had been shut-in with me for the last two years and knew not what changes the world outside had undergone in that time.

"Robo, call Otis," I said. "I gotta get outta this house."

Robo giggled and rushed to the phone in the kitchen. He returned and informed me that the cab would arrive in approximately thirty minutes.

"Well, we better get going," I said. "It's gonna take that long for me to make it to the road. I'm weak as a sick possum."

We left the house together, not bothering to lock the front door. I looked up at the sun, then at the path, and started walking. "C'mon, Robo," I said.

"I'm here," he answered. "To the road can you walk?"

"Just try to keep up," I replied.

Half an hour later, I was drenched with sweat, but had made it to where the cab would pick us up. It was the hardest thing I had ever done, but would go a long way toward my recuperation. I sat down on the grass under the oak tree nearest the road and leaned back against it and closed my eyes in the shade.

Seconds later, Otis pulled up in his vintage Checker cab. I smiled, sensing that something bigger than myself was at work here in Stringtown.

"Sweet home Aba-lama," I said with a chuckle as I struggled to my feet.

Robo rushed to help me into the cab. "Abalama," he repeated with a laugh.

"It's a joke," I said.

"As if I did not to know that, Mr. Yames."

The cab driver turned to size me up as I collapsed into his back seat. He hadn't seen me in two years, and I was the worse for wear. The tuck and roll in his taxi still looked good as new.

"Dang, mista, you been sick?"

"Yes, Otis. I've been sick and tired, and I'm sick and tired of it. But I'm getting better now. This is the first time I've been out in a couple of years."

"You ain't missed a thing. Relax. Where y'all wanna go?"

Robo sat down next to me – a little too close for heterosexual comfort.

"Anywhere, Otis," I said. "Take me some place you think someone who hasn't left the house in two years would want to go."

"I know the perfect place. What was y'all's name again, mista?"

"James Blank," I said, realizing I had not uttered my own name in forever. It felt like I was talking about someone other than myself.

***

We went to an old pig shack of a restaurant and got a mess of soul food, then went to a big park to eat at a concrete picnic table by a river. We sat on the table, rather than the concrete bench. We didn't talk as we ate. The food was too good for that. I could feel some of my strength and color coming back as the sun shone down on me.

"Okay, Otis," I said after we had finished. "Can you pick Robo up at the house tomorrow at ten in the morning?"

"Sho' nuff, Mista James, but ain't y'all comin' with?"

"Not up to it, Otis. I'm going to need some additional rest after today. I can only do so much."

"Yessir, Mista James. How long should I be expected to make myself available for the Robo?"

"The better part of the day, I think."

Otis took us back to the house, and I gave him a substantial tip. He confirmed the next day's appointment and drove away smiling.

***

Back at the house, I conferred with Robo.

"Okay, the first place I want you to go is the bank." I had a large legal pad and scrawled 'BANK' at the top of the page.

"And I am to cash yust these two checks, Mr. Yames?" Robo held two envelopes up.

"Yes, Robo. And if anyone asks why you're cashing them, rather than depositing, you say what?"

"I have a power of an attorney for dead O'Day lady. We must to fix old house to sell the estate."

"Perfect. What next?"

"I go to big box store."

"And you've got the list of items to purchase – the flat-screen, the computer, the stereo? And don't forget the DVD player and the movies I wrote down. And the compact discs."

"Yes, Mr. Yames. I am hoping the vehicle will contain it all."

"It'll be fine, Robo. That cab's got a giant trunk. Remember, you're coming back to the house to deliver those things before you leave again to the grocery store."

"Yes, to you I will come back. Then, to the grocery store I will go."

"And you have that list, as well?"

"I have made this list, Mr. Yames."

"Let me look at it, Robo."

"Mr. Yames, you must have some faith in your best of the friends."

"Too choleric, huh?" I muttered with a sly smile.

"You are getting better, Mr. Yames."

***

Robo and Otis completed the tasks without incident, other than the monumental persuasion it took to convince Otis to pull his cab all the way up to the house so we could unload the purchases. I ordered Robo to walk in front of the car waving a hundred dollar bill, like dangling a carrot in front of a mule.

That evening Robo and I set up the home theater in the downstairs living room. The concept of entertainment was something foreign in the old house. A television had never flickered within its lathe and plaster walls. Other than Robo's kitchen radio, the only source of entertainment the place had seen was my industrial-strength loofah.

"This is pretty much what you're going to be dealing with when you go out to find the band, Robo," I said as I loaded 'Spinal Tap' into the DVD player.

We watched the movie in silence. Robo glanced at me from time to time with wide eyes and gaping mouth, to which I responded simply with a knowing nod.

I had seen the movie so many times that I tuned it out, thinking instead about the guys in Mellowtron and Nicky Pepperonzi and The Loaves and Fishes and Da Dirty Third Warders and Lanny Kraywitz.

When the movie ended, Robo rose and turned on the overhead light. He looked at me and did a double-take. I was staring straight ahead with tears streaming down my cheeks and dripping off my chin. I was smiling, though.

"Mr. Yames! What is the matter please?"

"I'm happy, Robo. Come sit by me. I want to tell you stories."

I regaled Robo with epic tales through the night, until I saw the glow of the rising sun through the window's lace curtains.

"C'mon, Robo. Let's go out on the front porch and watch the sun rise. I haven't seen the sun come up since the last time I had some coke."

Robo looked puzzled, wondering why I would be up at dawn drinking soft drinks, but followed me outside.

The morning was magical. Everything glistened with condensed moisture. I gazed from left to right across the front yard, which was overgrown to the point of looking like a jungle. During my tenure with the debutante, it had been a manicured lawn worthy of a croquet or bocce tournament. I smiled as an idea sprouted in my newly fertile mind as to how I would shape up the yard. All I needed was a little manpower, or more accurately, bandpower.

Robo and I fell asleep and drowsed side-by-side until noon. I rose first and looked at my friend, who was sprawled in a very uncomfortable-looking position in his lounge chair. He was still asleep in REM-state, and his hands and legs kicked like a dreaming dog's. *He'll probably want me to rub his tummy when he wakes up*, I thought with a smile.

"Wake up, Robo!" I yelled. He jerked, suddenly conscious, wondering why he was on the porch.

"*Fetch* me some coffee, boy," I said and laughed at my own joke.

Robo was confused and disoriented, but he rose and crossed the porch to do my bidding.

"WAIT!" I yelled. Another old memory had just burst in my brain like a bottle rocket.

"Yes, Mr. Yames?" Robo asked.

"Do you know where that backpack I had when I first got here is?"

"Of course."

"Go to it and bring me my pipe and tobacco!"

A memory had come back of smoking a pipe in the early morning next to a highway. Scenes such as this were being recalled from deep inside my mind, but they were without context – like shards from a broken stained glass window. Each one was colorful, but there was a bigger picture I could not yet see. I was remembering and re-living individual thoughts and feelings, but there was a much larger story – a story I could not remember for the life of me.

CHAPTER FIVE

A man came and installed the cable TV and also the internet. The old house was slowly being dragged into the information age, but it wasn't going willingly. The poor cable guy was drilling holes all over the place and running wire like never before. Robo thanked him with carnitas tacos and a virgin mojito.

I was on the internet before the cable van had left the driveway, searching for 'Mellowtron'. I couldn't believe it when Google returned 1.7 million results. I went to the Wikipedia entry first and read it somberly.

***

Mellowtron was an American rock band made up of Cal E. Fornia on vocals, Headley Grange on guitar, Domino on bass, and The Sponge on drums and percussion. The band toured only one time – in a Winnebago driven by their manager, James Blank, now deceased.

The group released one well-received album, the self-titled 'Mellowtron', on Lanny Kraywitz' Lucite Records imprint. The record topped the Billboard album chart for six weeks and spawned the massive hits, 'Mick's Lips' and 'Juvenile's Grill', but Mellowtron never followed up on this chart success, instead imploding due to disagreements regarding musical direction, managerial decisions, and personal conflicts.

Unable to work together and abandoned by replacement manager, Nicky Pepperonzi, the band members were convinced by Lucite Records executives to release four individual solo albums as KISS did in 1978. The album covers featured air-brushed portraits of each member, but the effort was seen as a gimmick and sold terribly. The decision for each band member to play all the instruments on their solo album was a particularly bad move. Mellowtron disbanded, and the members went their separate ways shortly after this debacle.

The band's first and only tour was documented in the book, 'Band On The Run' by fan-turned-author, Matt Syverson. It was compiled from diary entries of original manager, James Blank.

(from Wikipedia)

***

The entry continued, but I read no further. I went to Amazon and found the book.

I laughed when I saw the Winnebago on the front and the image of Crisco in his kick drum on the back cover. I tried to be pissed off, but just smiled.

I ordered the novel to be overnighted C.O.D., for which I agreed to pay forty-two dollars over the cover price. I didn't care. It would be more than worth it to piece together the experiences I had somehow forgotten from my tour with Mellowtron. I had come to the conclusion that I had some weird and exotic form of amnesia, which allowed me to recall some memories vividly, but blocked any chronological specificity.

I surfed the web a bit more, but consciously avoided anything to do with Mellowtron. I would let the book tell me where I left off with the band, so I would now know where to begin.

***

The package arrived around noon the following day, and I jogged it upstairs. I was rebuilding my strength much faster than I was rebuilding my past, but the book was surely going to help.

I finished the memoir in a couple hours. It was a short book, but I found my life to be thoroughly entertaining. It sure as hell wasn't boring! I was pissed at Syverson for lifting my diary, but having re-lived through his book how I had ripped off Skunk, the record producer, as well as the promoter at the Texsun Festival, I decided I could forgive the greedy bastard.

Once I started reading, I could almost have closed my eyes and dictated. Every word came back to me from every diary entry, and I recalled the moment I wrote each one. I was transported through time and space to the time and place of each entry. It all came together in perfect chronological order.

I ran down the stairs and found Robo in the 'Workout' room on the StairMaster. I stifled a laugh when I saw what he was wearing. "Get off," I commanded. Robo stepped off the contraption, and I took 'Band On The Run' and shoved it into the top of his left leg-warmer. "Read this book right away, Robo."

"Yes, Mr. Yames!"

Robo high-stepped off to read the diary. I boarded the StairMaster and increased the resistance so I could blast my calves and quads.

Three hours later, Robo returned to the Workout room and found me tangled in the machine.

"Mr. Yames, what to yourself have you done?"

"I'm broken, Robo. Fix me."

Robo helped me out of the machine and to the kitchen, where we would once again eat and talk.

"I made chili relleno for the dinner, Mr. Yames. I will hope you like it!"

"It looks wonderful, my friend," I said as I looked at the 10-inch long, bright red pepper on my plate. Its skin was blistered, and taco meat brimmed forth from a slit down the length of it.

"In my country, this is to be called 'The Devil's Dingus', Mr. Yames."

"What wonderful traditions you have," I said. "It's smoking hot, though, Robo. Let's let it cool down for a minute. What did you think of the book?"

"Mr. Matt a very good writer is. You too, Mr. Yames."

"What about the band, Robo? Did you learn anything?"

I learned many and much about all of you. I feel I know you as well as my littermates."

Was this guy raised by wolves? I wondered, but didn't explore the thought further.

"Okay, good," I said. "After we eat the Devil's penis, we'll look at the internet together and see what we can learn. It's almost time for you to go."

After dinner, Robo and I sat in front of the computer together, watching YouTube videos of Mellowtron performing at the Synesthesia club in their masks, in Vegas at the lounge in the Imperial Palace, and at The Joint, among others. I hadn't been aware all these clandestine recordings were taking place at the time, but they were wonderful to watch now. There was even footage of the performance at the Texsun Festival and the Winnebago getting blown up afterward.

Finally, it was time to hit the sack. I yawned and stretched my arms and said, "Robo, get ready to sign a bunch of checks in the morning. I need a bank account full of money."

***

I won't lie and tell you I did the following without pangs from a guilty conscience. The next morning, I opened every one of those checks we had sorted and made Robo sign them to be deposited into a new bank account, called 'Mellowtron, LLC'. I spent years with the old debutante and never heard a word from any of her relatives, if she had any. Robo and I seemed to be her only family – at least that's what I convinced myself. We deserved at least a part of her wealth. We deserved all of it, I guess you could say.

Otis took us to the bank, and it went much smoother than I expected. Nobody questioned us or even raised an eyebrow. I guess when 1.2 million dollars comes into a bank on a Wednesday morning during a recession it isn't likely to be turned away. The crazy thing was – there was still another large bag of checks at the house, not to mention the old dame's jewelry, antiques, and other personal effects. I decided to leave the jewelry and other material possessions untouched in case the old bitch's family showed up. The checks had never been deposited in any of the old lady's accounts, so nobody would ever know they existed. I felt like a Goodfella, which brought a thought of my friend, Nicky Pepperonzi, which brought a sad smile.

I was punch-drunk on the ride home. It felt surreal, like I was a boxer who took a dive in the third for a big payoff from Don King. I recalled the guilt I felt when we seized five grand from that slimy Texsun Festival promoter – chump change. I was a millionaire now, even though I had been an eggplant for the last two years. Funny how things work out.

***

Finally, the day came to send little Robo out into the world. We stood on the porch together early in the morning. Robo reminded me of a kid with a satchel getting ready to catch the bus to first grade. He was happy and nervous and a bundle of other emotions, which all added up to sheer terror – kind of like the feeling of riding a nasty roller coaster for the first time.

We were waiting on the porch for Otis.

"Oh, Mr. Yames, what if I am to forget something."

"Not a chance. We went over the list a dozen times. You're going to be fine, Tiny Dancer."

Robo smiled. The Elton John song was one of his favorites.

"I am to go to The Sponge, first, Mr. Yames?"

"Yes, just like we discussed, Robo. There's nothing to be afraid of. I have a good idea where he'll be. When you find him, lay back and observe. I'll let you know when to make your move."

"Then I am to Taser him!"

"Not so fast, Dirty Harry. First you talk to him. I told you how to bribe people. If that doesn't work, use the Taser. Or, if you can come up with a better plan, feel free. I trust you, Robo."

"I can't wait, Mr. Yames, but I am to be so nervous! Will you be being okay without Mr. Robo?"

"I'll survive, lil' buddy. I'm tougher than I look. I've got everything I need, and I can call Otis at any time. Don't worry about Mr. James – worry about yourself."

Otis pulled up at the end of the driveway and waved to me. He saw Robo in his pastel outfit and shook his head, smiling.

"Mr. Yames!" Robo said, terrified at the last moment.

I wrapped my arms around him for one final hug, then pushed him away. "Run, Robo! You're going to have the time of your little life! Run, Robo, run!"

Robo rushed away with one hand carrying his laptop briefcase and the other his Batman suitcase.

"Godspeed, you glorious imbecile," I whispered.

Robo skipped to the cab and jumped in the back. Otis drove away slowly, and I sat down on the porch steps and wept.

CHAPTER SIX

Robo was gone, and I was without companionship for the first time in, well, forever. I sat and thought for a couple hours, attempting to come to terms with all I had remembered and all I had learned in the last week.

This hadn't been easy on me, but I had internalized my emotions until now, not wanting to appear weak in front of Robo. Without warning, everything manifested in a terrific tantrum. I laughed until I cried, screaming torrents at the heavens, then sobbed in pain until I collapsed in exhaustion.

I don't know what drove me to it, but I suddenly wanted to evaluate my life even more deeply. My time with Mellowtron was now clear, but the time before that was still murky. I was too young for a mid-life crisis, but something similar was happening to me. Please forgive my ego, but the best comparison I can make is to the crucifixion and resurrection of Jesus Christ. My old self had figuratively died over the last two years, and a new James Blank was rising from some symbolic passing. This process may have a name, but I doubt it. From what I've read, an individual torturing himself in this manner is usually done in South America after the ingestion of an hallucinogenic rainforest concoction under the guidance of a shaman. I guess I'll call it 'soul-stripping' – kind of like removing some really well-stuck wallpaper from the inside of one's own skull. The process took two weeks.

In this meditative state, I realized my life had consisted of wild swings, from being completely dependent as a child, to being a caretaker of the debutante, to being a controlling master of Mellowtron, then back to being wholly dependent on precious Robo. It was almost as if I had already gone through the cradle to grave process by the relatively young age of twenty-seven. There was something deep inside me, from my past, that had guided my behavior and the choices I made, and I wanted to find it. I squeezed into my mental hip waders and went deeper, searching for suppressed and repressed memories, dropping glowing crumbs of plutonium into the swampy water to help me find my way back.

Childhood memories filtered back to me slowly as the bricks of my wall were shoveled aside like the rubble of bombed-out London. I listened to Lou Reed's 'Berlin' album repeatedly during this self-psychoanalysis, especially the song 'Kids', which brought back taxidermied memories of my parents. I also listened to John Lennon's 'Mother' on repeat and primal screamed for hours. I still couldn't remember the name of my elementary school, but it definitely wasn't 'Strawberry Fields'.

At one point, I staggered to the nearest bathroom and confronted myself in the mirror. I wanted to rip my own face off like the guy in 'Poltergeist' and view the real me. I saw my reflection, which I barely recognized, and punched it and it shattered. In a panic, I referenced the 3"x5" card file in my head, searching for the closest approximation of my childhood, and found a card labeled, 'The Who, Tommy'. I raced to the computer with a bleeding hand and crammed 'the who tommy' into Google and watched YouTube clips from the movie until I fell asleep on the floor near dawn.

As I slept, I dreamed of my childhood.

***

My mother had wanted a girl, so she responded to my birth with mixed feelings. When I was alone with her she raised me like a pageant child – thankfully as a prince, rather than a princess. I was too young to object, but I loved the attention, regardless. My mother suffered from 'spells', though. I don't know if they were migraines or some sort of addiction, but during these episodes she turned me over to my father, 'Coach'. She had these spells a lot, so my time was split fairly evenly between my parents.

Coach was what you might call the supreme hard-ass of all time, and he showed me no mercy. He was an unsympathetic sadist, hiding the shame of his frequent impotence behind a flattop haircut and double-knit, high-waisted coaching shorts. He had me doing 'toughness drills' before I was out of diapers. He would pinch me, and if I cried he pinched me harder. If I didn't cry, I got a little piece of beef jerky, which was really a dog treat meant for Coach's bulldog, Hamstring, but I didn't know that.

Coach treated my mother even worse. He eventually drove her to commit suicide during one of her spells. Coach had been especially mean to her that day – he wanted to go golfing, rather than babysit me, and he let her know it physically. Beaten into submission, she snuck away to kill herself in the bathtub, so she wouldn't stain the carpet. In desolate desperation, she sawed at her left wrist with a butter knife, but the blade was too dull to do more than mar her ivory skin. What she did next is almost as painful to write as it was to remember.

I'll just say it. My mother bit into her own wrist and ripped it wide open. She let out a shriek upon realizing what she had done, which brought me running to the bathroom. My loving mom looked at me with sad terror and defeat in her eyes – blood was running down her chin. I ran to her and stepped into the tub and she hugged me tight, until her arms were inanimate weight upon me. I laid there for an hour, crying softly and talking to my mother for the last time.

I did not speak for weeks after the incident, even when people at the funeral tried to console me and tell me my life would be happy. Afterward, my father blamed me for what had happened, since my mother had wanted a daughter so badly. I didn't understand – I was only four.

One day not long after my mother's passing, I stood in front of my father, red welts across my soft arms and puffy cheeks. Coach had pinched me dozens of times, trying to get a response.

"Speak, Godammit!"

I said nothing, and I didn't cry. I was in a mental place where my father couldn't inflict any more pain on me. I was mute and devoid of emotion, just like Townshend's Tommy. Coach grabbed my ears and pulled them away from my head with all his strength. "Can't you hear me, retard?!" He shook my whole body, and it felt as if my ears would tear off.

My father loosened his hold and picked me up roughly by the shoulders. I was small for my age, and I balled up in fetal position. Coach hurled me across the room like a fastball. I skipped across the tile floor and crashed in a wad under my bed. Our housekeeper, Melba, rushed into the room and pulled me out. Melba was our new maid, a black lady about thirty-years-old, hired to take up the slack around the house in the absence of my mother. Coach couldn't butter toast, much less clean and do laundry and take care of a child. Melba hadn't liked the vibe around the house, but she had endured it in silence, thinking my mother's suicide was the cause of the tension.

Now she spoke forcefully to Coach. "You gone and done it now, mister man! You gonna be arrested right quick if you don't get the hell outta here! Leave this poor child alone! He ain't done a thing wrong!"

I whimpered and clutched Melba tight.

"Now git, before I call the po-lice! May God have mercy on you, you son of a bitch! Don't come back until you a real man!"

That was the last I saw of Coach and Hamstring. Melba took me home and raised me as her own from that day forward, alongside six children of her own who varied widely in age. I never knew the father of my new brothers and sisters, but there was a man named Wilson who was around most of the time. He had a gentle nature and lived next door. He never spent the night, but he was around Melba's house from early morning until bedtime when he wasn't at work at a tire shop.

***

I woke and was apoplectic at the recovery of this painful period in my life, but now the bricks I was removing from my wall started getting lighter. Thoughts of happiness washed over me. I remembered my adoptive family playing music together and dancing and singing. Melba would pound out ragged, slightly out of tune chords on an old piano as my brothers and sisters and I clapped and stomped our feet and sang as loud as we could, dogs howling and jumping with us. I remembered turning ropes while my sisters double-dutched and chanted jump-rope rhymes. We were happy. My tears of pain turned into tears of joy.

I lifted myself from the floor, at peace with this part of my past. This was enough for now.

"I need a dose of Led Zeppelin," I said. "I've been weak long enough. It's time to be strong."

I put on Led Zep's first album and cranked up the speakers. I blasted through the entire compact disc without blinking. I was in a trance, trying to process all of it – my childhood, my adult life, the last two years. I was just getting started. I played every Zeppelin album in order and sang and danced and body-rocked right along with every track. Every time John Bonham hit his snare drum it blasted away part of the shell that confined me. I had spent a lot of time remembering my past – now I remembered what rock and roll was and what rock and roll meant to people like me.

***

This went on through the day and through the next night. At some point the phone rang, and I talked to and advised Robo, though I did not turn down the music. I had transitioned from Zep to The Flying Burrito Brothers to David Bowie to The Stones to The Beatles and was absorbed in 'She Came In Through The Bathroom Window'. I wasn't under the influence of any substance, but I was intoxicated by the music I had gone without for so long. Eventually, I passed out on the entry way beside the front door.

Some time later, a knock on the door interrupted my stupor. 'Her Majesty' was playing softly, repeating over and over. I went back into deep sleep, thinking I was imagining something. Another knock blasted through the door like someone was trying to open it by force.

I rose to my feet, disoriented. I didn't feel resurrected at the moment. I felt like a deflated blimp. I opened the door, expecting nothing.

"Holy shit."

"Sponge!"

I reached to my old friend, but could not catch him. He fainted and did the Nestea plunge right there on the front porch, which bashed and gashed his noggin something terrible when he hit the nearly petrified oak floor. I dragged him inside and rushed to the bathroom to get a towel. I returned and placed it under his head and went to the kitchen to find an ice-pack.

I hustled back and applied a bag of frozen peas to Sponge's head and tried to aid and comfort my old drummer friend. He was injured and confused.

"James, I can play the gig," he said as he struggled to

his feet.

"There's no gig," I replied as I supported him.

"Let's record another take, then," he said and collapsed to the floor.

I helped him up and led him to the 'Royal Crown' bedroom and put him to bed.

I went to the kitchen to make breakfast. I hadn't eaten in forever. The phone rang.

"Hello," I answered.

"I have determined that you are paying too much for auto insurance," a robotic voice said.

"Screw you! I don't even own a car." I slammed the phone down on the receiver. My hash browns were on the verge of becoming hash blacks.

The phone rang again.

"I thought I told you to shove it!"

"Happy birthday, Mr. Yames!"

"Robo, I'm sorry! What's going on? Sponge just got here! Where are you?"

"Mr. Yames, you are now twenty-eight! I wish I could to be there with you!"

"Thanks, Robo," I said with a smile. "What's up?"

"I told Mr. Sponge he would have a haven at the house in Alabama. So many of the people are after him."

"You did good, Robo. He's here." I didn't know what his last statement had meant, but I figured I'd have a better chance of understanding it by talking to Sponge. "Where are you, Robo?"

"I in Los Angeles! The Big Apple!"

I smiled and asked Robo who he was going after next, although I had a strong suspicion.

"I will talk to Mr. California next, Mr. Yames."

The sound of planes landing and taking off made

conversing with Robo difficult.

"Good luck, Mr. Yames!"

"I think that's what I'm supposed to say to you, Robo." The connection was cut and a dial tone replaced Robo's happy voice. The old land-line phone in my hand felt weird after using a cell phone for all of my adult life – like I had been talking into Alexander Graham Bell's femur. I hung up the bone.

"That was strange," I said. "As if everything else around here isn't. Things must be getting back to normal."

I grabbed a piece of bacon and looked out the kitchen window as I took a bite, smiling as I chewed.

"Wonder who'll be arriving next?" I said.

CHAPTER SEVEN

I gazed down at Sponge, who was sleeping peacefully. I was sitting in a high-backed rocking chair next to his bed, re-reading 'Personality Plus' and 'Band On The Run', preparing for what lay before me.

Sponge looked the same, other than having gained a few pounds and appearing somewhat more mature, which is kind of a joke when you're talking about someone who has never held a job. He had crow's feet around his eyes that weren't there before and crease lines in his forehead. Of all the things he'd been injecting, Botox was not one of them.

Without warning, Sponge opened his eyes and looked at me. "Why did you make us think you were dead, James?" he said flatly.

"I didn't. I think Nicky did that, but I haven't talked to him."

"You just left us then."

"Well, someone close to me passed away, and I kind of had a nervous breakdown or something. I'm better now."

"That doesn't make it right. We couldn't do a thing without you – that's the way you always wanted it. You never let us do a thing for ourselves. Then you left us. How do you think that worked out?"

"I'm sorry, Sponge. Believe me, things haven't been good in my world, either. I want things to be different this time."

"What do you mean 'this time'? We've all moved on to bigger and better things."

"Are you serious? What are you doing now?"

"Living off royalties."

"Sounds wonderful," I said.

"Not really, James. I made eleven thousand dollars last

year. Not to mention all the people making my life a living hell."

"I know about the album's success," I said. "You should be living like a rock star. I read the Lucite contract before we signed it. You're rich!"

"Well, we *didn't* read it, James. I mean we didn't read the re-worked contract Lucite made us sign before the album came out. The label execs said that since we broke up when you disappeared, we were technically not the same band that signed the first contract. They convinced us you had been ripping us off, too. They said they were working in our best interests."

"Bastards!" I cursed. "And you believed them!" That cut deep, since I had always looked out for the boys as if they were my own flesh and blood and attempted to shield them from music business vultures. "What about Nicky Pepperonzi? Is he crooked or what?"

"Couldn't tell ya. After he supposedly buried you, he came back to New York and disappeared. He told someone the mob was out to get him. Never heard from him again."

"So you had no manager or other adviser from then on?"

"Not unless you count Crisco. Our business decisions were made by a straight up-or-down vote. That wasn't the best way to do it."

I didn't respond. Sponge was obviously wrung out, if you'll pardon the pun. I didn't want to burden him too heavily so soon after his arrival.

"Why am I here, James?" he asked.

"Good question. I haven't really worked that out, but I've really missed you, if that counts for anything."

"Doesn't count for much. You abandoned us."

"That's gonna take a while for you to get past, huh?"

"Yep."

"I tried to save your life at the Texsun Festival."

"I know. Then you abandoned me."

"Go back to sleep, Sponge. I think the head trauma is affecting your thinking."

I exited the R.C. bedroom and closed the door softly, glad to be away from Sponge's accusing memory. I felt bad – I hadn't much considered the effects of my sudden departure on Mellowtron. Things had not gone well for them, to say the least.

I sat on the bottom step of the stairs to think, but nothing much came to me except guilt. Guilt was not going to help me. I stood up and walked to the entertainment room and sat down at the computer.

"YouTube, put a bullet in my brain," I said. I wasn't suicidal. I wanted to use the internet to spark ideas and creativity in my mind without actually having to think for myself. Sounds like an oxymoron, but that's the way it works for me.

I closed my eyes, and my fingers typed. I can automatic type like some psychics can automatic write. I think my output is more worthwhile. I turned off my mind and let my fingers do the walking. When I opened my eyes, I was happy to see the words 'Van Halen Diver Down' in the YouTube search box.

"The rock gods have spoken," I said. I laughed and pushed 'enter', and a multitude of selections popped up. I turned it over to something bigger than myself and clicked 'Where Have All The Good Times Gone!'.

That was a wonderful starting point. I listened to the song and meditated. Next, I listened to 'Dancing in the Street' and envisioned a glorious future and smiled. I clicked on 'Little Guitars' and let the music envelope me while I meditated good thoughts. *This must be magic*, I told myself.

I heard a knock at the front door. I rushed over and opened it, expecting Cal.

A smoking hot, stacked redhead in a nurse's uniform stood before me. She had legs that went all the way down to her clear plastic stripper shoes.

"You James?"

"Y-y-yes," I stammered. "Who are you?"

"My name's Cherry Topping. The little bald guy told me to come here – Rainbow or whatever his name was."

"You mean Robo. He's my manservant."

"That's him. Nice guy. Weird, but nice. He told me I absolutely had to come see you. He paid me, actually. You gonna invite me in or what?"

"Of course! Have a seat in the parlor, and I'll get us something to drink. Be right back."

Cherry made herself comfortable, and I rushed to pour some lemonade for us. I attempted to impress her by garnishing both glasses with a maraschino cherry. I was struggling to remember how to be suave around a lady, but it had been a *long* time. I wished I had showered this month.

"To what do I owe the honor of your visit, Cherry?" I said as I sat down on the opposite side of the old sofa from her.

"You tell me, James. I couldn't understand half of what the little bald guy said. He sure was excited."

"I'll bet."

"He told me it was urgent and that Mellowtron was reuniting and that you needed my help. He handed me a thousand bucks and a plane ticket and gave me your address here in Alabama. I was curious, so here I am."

"And I'm so glad you came, Cherry! But I'm still confused. Where did Robo find you?"

"At the Whisky a Go-Go on the Sunset Strip. That's where I was performing."

"Ah, you're a musician," I said.

"I'm an entertainer. I was the opening act for the Cal E. Fornia Experience. Cal didn't show up the night your little friend met me."

"That doesn't sound like him," I said, concerned.

"Yeah, right. The dude's a total flake. He's a nice guy, ya know, but he's depressed. I feel sorry for him. He's really lost. Plus, most of the crowd are only coming to the club to see me, anyway. I have to perform before *and* after Cal's set, just so the people won't leave when his band plays. They stay to see me."

"What do you do?"

"Well, I got this stage persona, 'Boobnanza'. It's a bit over the top, really, but it pays the bills, so whaddya gonna do?"

"Boobnanza?"

"Yeah, Boobnanza. There's a guy who introduces me with a real big voice, ya know? He's like, '*Boobnanza-nanza-nanza! She's the Titanic of the tit world with the biggest life preservers in the bizness!*' It's corny, but the guys like it."

"I'll bet," I said. I noticed I was drooling on the sofa, so I moved my leg to cover it before Cherry could see.

"Well, I'm here, James," she said. "Now what?"

"Good question, Cherry. I hadn't expected anyone other than the band members. We've got lots of room if you want to stay, but it's up to you. You might be bored here. Are you really a nurse?"

"I'm no nurse, but I can definitely make you feel better, James, if you know what I mean." She laughed in a very unladylike manner. I wasn't nervous around her any more.

She was like one of the guys. "I'm joking, James. I'm no slut."

"Thank goodness," I said, trying to mask my disappointment. "Well, Miss Topping, how 'bout you pick a room and stay for a while? You're already here, so you might as well enjoy yourself for a week or two."

"I might as well, right James?" Her full lips smiled brightly, and my heart fluttered, causing me to nearly faint.

***

"She's hot," Sponge said. "What would you call the color of that bikini?"

"Apricot."

We were looking down at Cherry from the window of Sponge's bedroom. She was sunbathing next to the non-functioning fountain in the backyard.

"What's been happening with you since I left, Sponge?" My gaze did not stray from Boobnanza and neither did his.

"Apricot, huh?"

"Sponge, are you listening to me?"

Sponge just gurgled, so I took him by the arm and led him into a sitting room with a view of the *front* yard. I figured looking down on overgrown vegetation would be more conducive to our discussion than trying to determine if Cherry's hedge was pruned.

There were two small sofas that faced each other across a round coffee table. More than likely, this was the first use the room had seen in decades.

"Pretty good place for a meeting, huh?" I asked Sponge.

"Good as any," Sponge said curtly. He was still pissed at me for disappearing two years before.

I looked down at the kudzu-covered vegetation and half-smiled like a baseball player that has just had strike three called on him for a ball that was clearly outside.

"Sponge, you've got to realize I didn't intentionally hurt you."

"I think you sabotaged Mellowtron, James, in some passive-aggressive way."

"Sponge, the love of my life was dying. I never even got to tell her goodbye."

Sponge looked at me, wide-eyed. "The old debutante? I thought you hated her! You always called her 'the old bitch'."

"I had a resentment toward her for firing me. But I never would have discovered Mellowtron if she hadn't. I think she wanted me to find myself. You're the only one who knows the truth." I bowed my head in humiliation. "Hate me if you want, but it was something I had to do – I had to come back here. I'm sorry I didn't explain it to you." The floodgates opened, and I sobbed, humiliating myself further.

Sponge rose and moved to a spot on the sofa next to me. "Well, that changes things. I'm sorry, James. I guess I've only been seeing my side of the story. You know I love you. I can't hold a grudge." He hugged me, and I rested my head on his shoulder.

I spoke into his neck. "I can't fix the past. I can only make amends and move forward."

"Aw, James," he said. "I understand. Let's figure out how we're gonna fix this thing. Stop crying."

I pulled away from him, tears all over the place. "You mean you forgive me?"

"Hell, yeah. You're James Blank – the best manager in the freakin' world! You took Mellowtron from a crappy garage band to the most popular act on the planet!"

I smiled like an orphan who has just been adopted by Bill Gates.

"Let's take some lemonade out to the chick in the apricot bikini, Sponge."

"That's the first great idea you've had in your second term as band manager."

We went downstairs and gave Cherry her drink and stood by the dried-up fountain.

"Why don't you put water in this thing?" Sponge asked after he launched a healthy loogie into it.

"That fountain didn't hold water ten years ago," I said.

Sponge reached in his pocket for a pack of cigarettes and offered me one.

"No thanks," I said. "Gave 'em up."

He reached in another pocket and produced a purple lighter with a pink skull on it.

"That's just like the lighter you used to have," I said. I questioned my memory. "Isn't it?"

"It *is* the lighter, James. It still works."

"But hasn't it been something like two years since you guys saw each other?" Cherry asked.

"Yep," said Sponge.

"It's obviously a refillable lighter, Cherry," I said.

Sponge smiled slyly. "Nope."

Cherry and I looked at each other, trying to understand.

"Okay," I said. "You're telling me that you've had the same lighter for over two years, and it's never run out."

"Exactly. Jedediah Kanobi gave it to me. It's the 'eternal flame'."

"That's crazy!" said Cherry, and we all laughed.

"Everything about Mellowtron is," I said.

CHAPTER EIGHT

The next morning I had a business meeting with Sponge. I didn't have any sort of agenda. I just wanted to get started doing something productive. We were in the second floor sitting room where we talked the day before, now referred to as the 'second floor office'.

I took a sip of my coffee and got to the point. "Sponge, what drugs are you on, and how much is your habit?"

"I'm clean and sober, James."

I spit my coffee, but was able to direct it through the open window, rather than at Sponge.

"You don't need to lie to me. Let me see your arms."

"There aren't any track marks, James. I'm serious – I'm clean, except for cigs. You can blame that on the eternal flame," he said with a laugh.

A sunbeam could have knocked me over. I mumbled, "I'm proud of you. Tell me more."

"James, I went home after the tour fully expecting to fall back in my usual routine, but it was a different world. Every guy I'd ever shared a doobie with came out of the woodwork and wanted to be my best friend."

"Hangers-on," I said, my face pinched like I had bitten into an unripe persimmon.

"Exactly. And that wasn't the worst of it. There were people following me everywhere I went."

"Paparazzi," I hissed with an even more gruesome expression on my face. "Leeches!"

"It wasn't photographers, James. It was protesters. They latched onto me like a Gila monster."

"Protesting what?"

"First it was PETA. Finally, I stopped wearing my leather pants and boots and they quit, but the Westside

Baptist Church picked up right where they left off."

"Why were they picketing you?"

"Why *weren't* they, James? Drugs, alcohol, sex, rock and roll, driving an SUV, irresponsible use of a teenager – you name it. They made my life miserable until your little friend helped me out."

"Good old Robo!" I said, beaming like a proud father. "What happened?"

"Well, he infiltrated the Westside people, but he stood out like a sore thumb. His sign said 'You Are To Be Ashamed'. One day I was backing my Suburban up at a liquor store, and he jumped into the passenger seat. He had a black plastic gun that looked real. He put it to my head and made me drive by the protestors. They cheered like crazy. I guess they thought he was going to execute me. He made me drive away, and I wasn't followed for the first time in weeks. He apologized and told me I had to come here, but he didn't tell me anything else. I sure as hell wasn't expecting to see you."

"So why did you come?"

"He rescued me. I had nothing to lose. I've had a hard time making decisions since you left, James. Can we leave it at that?"

"Of course. I'm sorry Robo did that, but I'm glad it got you here."

"Me, too."

There was a soft knock at the door, and Cherry popped her luscious head in. "Coffee need a warm-up, guys? I hope I'm not interrupting anything important."

"Come in!" Sponge and I gushed simultaneously.

Cherry had her nurse uniform on and luxuriously refilled our coffee cups and stirred cream into them. I think she was starved for attention, since she hadn't performed her

Boobnanza act lately.

"Pour yourself a cup, Cherry, and join us," I said.

"Oh, I don't want to intrude on your business meeting."

"It's fine," Sponge said. "We're just catching up on old times."

"Well, you two carry on as if I wasn't here."

Sponge and I caught each others' glance, and our eyes told dirty jokes to each other. It was as if we had never said goodbye.

"Have you kept in contact with the rest of the guys?" I asked Sponge.

"Nope. We agreed to talk in ten years to see if we wanna do a reunion. None of us wanted to even look at each other after all the bullshit that went down after you died."

"God, I'm so sorry," I said.

"Don't apologize again, James." Sponge's voice was stern, and he looked me in the eye. I saw that he had changed, just as I had. If the other guys had undergone similar transformations, the new Mellowtron was going to be as serious as Marines going into battle. Gone were the days when I would tell people what to do and have them follow blindly. I would be explaining things from now on and taking input.

Sensing the tension, Cherry spoke. "What can I do to help, guys? I can't just lay around all the time looking beautiful."

Our eyes met again, and Sponge and I tried to keep our brains out of the gutter.

"Well, what are you good at?" I asked.

"I used to be a Zumba instructor."

"Well, that'll be good for our health regimen. Anything else?" I asked.

"I know!" she exclaimed. She rushed off and returned a

minute later carrying a clipboard that must have been part of her nurse costume.

"I can take notes," she said. "I love to handwrite! It's all about the penmanship."

"Excellent," I said. "This is all going swimmingly. Cherry, please note the date and that this is meeting one of Mellowtron, Phase Two. The first agenda item has been discussed, and Sponge is NOT on drugs."

"Duly noted, sir."

"And we *will* exact revenge on the Westside Baptist Church," Sponge added.

"Also noted," Cherry said. "I hate those bastards."

We all laughed and paused to sip our coffee.

"Is Robo going to find the other guys?" Sponge asked, growing serious. "I'm worried there's gonna be hard feelings when we all get together again."

"He's supposed to track everyone down. That's the plan, anyway. I've gotta be honest, though – I didn't really give him any instructions other than loose ideas about where you guys might be. I left the rest up to him. I haven't been much of a decision maker lately, either. I've been completely dependent on Robo for the last two years."

"That doesn't sound like you, James."

"I know. I've changed – a lot. Which reminds me – I'm working on my health. This meeting is now adjourned. Let's go for a walk, guys. I can't neglect my regimen. Nurse Cherry, I hope you don't mind applying my sunscreen."

"Of course not, Mr. Blank."

"I'm gonna need some, too," Sponge added with a sly smile.

***

The three of us left the house at ten and walked the rest of the morning. We didn't set out on the road in front of the house. I thought that might attract unwanted attention. We left through the backyard and walked through fields of grass and plowed dirt, climbing over or under fences when we encountered them. We saw houses in the distance, but consciously veered away from them. Sponge and Cherry were happy to be away from the bustle and hustle of the city. My lungs were appreciative for the fresh air, and in a managerial sense, I saw this as a team-building exercise. I was thinking differently now. So many bands spend their lives holed up in dank, smokey basements in the daytime and dank, smokey clubs at night. I guess I was finally coming around, like Alice Cooper before me – get out on the golf course and knock a few balls around once in a while and get out of the dungeon.

We sang Beatles songs as we strolled together. We picked and ate berries from a mulberry tree we found until our fingers and tongues were stained black. We set out toward home and trekked along the edge of a plowed field. I spotted something and pointed it out to my friends.

"An arrowhead!" Cherry cried. "Can I have it, James? I'm part Cherokee."

"Of course you are," I said. I picked it up and saw that it was made of iron-laced red flint. "It's yours."

Cherry took the two inch point from my hand and held it up to the sun. "Oh, James!" She kissed me on the cheek, which felt like a punch from Clubber Lang.

We made it home, and Nurse Cherry made sandwiches and limeades for us. I was thoroughly enjoying having her around, as was Sponge. After we ate, we all went to our chosen bedrooms and took a nap.

***

Once again, there was a knock at the front door. I happened to be awake, staring at the ceiling and daydreaming, so I got up and hurried downstairs. I assumed it would be Cal. I was excited to finally see him in all his trashy magnificence.

I opened the door to find a guy in a wheelchair staring back at me. He was slender and tan, around fifty years old. I recognized the scent of English Leather. His hair was pulled back in a once-fashionable short ponytail, and his beard was as stubbly as a re-run of 'Miami Vice'. He had a Led Zeppelin shirt on, and actually resembled Robert Plant in a way. He had 'music business' written all over him, but I couldn't tell if he was more promoter or more roadie. A beat-up car I recognized as a 1971 Dodge Charger Super Bee was parked near the porch. It was purple with orange accents and numerous dents.

He stood up from his chair and extended his hand. "I'm Mike the Microphone. You must be James Blank."

"Yes. Microphone. James," I said. I was bewildered. He had gone from disabled to abled right in front of me.

"Who are you?" I asked.

"I'm Mike the Microphone."

"I got that. Let me be more specific – why are you here?"

"Robo told me to come."

"Okay, but *why* did he tell you to come?" I felt like a dentist trying to extract the meaning of life from Stephen Hawking's wisdom teeth.

"I'm your new recording engineer," he said with a toothy smile. The guy was cheerful, at least.

I stepped toward Mike, and he moved aside. I sat down in his wheelchair. "Well, you *could* push me inside," I said. "Since you woke me from a nap."

Sponge was walking down the stairs as we entered. He stopped and asked, "Are you hurt, James?"

"Nope, just confused."

"That makes two of us," he said.

Mike the Mike spoke, somewhat exasperated. "Guys, I'm Mike the Microphone. I'm your new recording engineer. It couldn't be simpler."

"Sure, that's simple," I said. "But what makes you qualified to do that, and what's up with the steel wheelchair?"

"You mean you don't know who I am?" he asked incredulously.

Sponge and I looked at each other and made 'who is this guy?' faces. Nothing surprised us any more after all we'd been through, but we weren't very trusting of strangers.

Mike looked irritated. "Show me to your internet!"

I led him to the entertainment den and let him do as he pleased.

"There! Read it and Wiki-weep!" he said after a minute of Googling.

Sponge and I looked over Mike's shoulders and read his Wikipedia page. He patiently scrolled down as we did so.

"You're a famous bootlegger?" I asked

"I'm a taper. Bootleggers make moonshine."

"It says your wheelchair is a recording unit. Is that true?" Sponge said.

"Yep. I recorded a number of famous live recordings with it – *in stereo*."

"Well, that's cool and all," Sponge said. "But why are you here if you have such a prolific and successful career as a taper?"

"You're the drummer for Mellowtron, right?" Mike asked.

"Used to be."

"That's why I'm here. I've recorded the best jam bands

of all time, but I've never captured a Mellowtron show."

"You ever heard of the Loaves and Fishes?" I asked.

"Of course I have! I've been following and taping them on their current tour. They're opening for Rush right now. I met Robo in the crowd at the L.A. Forum show. The little guy couldn't see over the crowd, so I let him stand in my wheelchair while I recorded the Loaves."

"Weren't you there to record Rush?" I asked.

"Hell no! They're good and all, but the Loaves are out of this world. They're spiritual."

"Yeah, we know," I said.

"So why did you come here?" Sponge asked.

"To tape you guys. Like I said – I never got to catch Mellowtron live."

"Mellowtron is a long way from playing shows," I said. "I mean, the band is broken up."

"Not for long is what that Robo guy said, and he was very convincing. If Mellowtron is getting back together, I want to be in on it. The live shows will come in time. Remember – I'm a recording engineer. I'm a studio expert. You guys are gonna need one."

Sponge looked at me and smiled.

"Sponge, I gotta ask you something serious," Mike said.

"What?"

"How in holy hell did you get that kick drum sound on your album? I've never heard anything like it."

"Crisco," Sponge said with a grin as he side-eyed me.

"What the...?"

I interrupted, stifling a laugh. "Mike, find yourself a bedroom that's not being used, then come to the kitchen. Park your wheelchair wherever you like."

Mike wandered off, pushing his chair and mumbling softly, "Crisco?"

***

Fifteen minutes later, the four of us sat drinking coffee in the kitchen. Nothing more than small talk took place, but Cherry had pen in hand, memorializing everything we had to say. It looked like Matt Syverson wasn't going to be writing the next chapter of Mellowtron.

"Okay, guys," I said. "I've been laying around dormant for the last two years. I'm ready to get things done, but I don't want to rush you, if you're not. I hope you don't mind me hijacking what should be a casual meeting of the minds. If there are two or more of us together, I think we should be working – or at least thinking about the future. Planning."

"We understand," said Cherry without taking her eyes from the notes she was taking.

I reached over and gripped the top of her clipboard between my index finger and thumb and guided it down flat against the table. "It'll be a lot easier to write like this," I said. I was really just trying to get a better look at her chest.

Cherry laughed. "I'm new at this, James. I'm a nurse, not a secretary!"

"Of course you are," I said.

"Okay," I continued. "How confident are you guys that Mellowtron is going to reunite? Think the rest of the guys are gonna show up?"

Sponge responded first. "Domino will be here if that Robo dude tells him he talked to me."

"Are you absolutely sure?" I asked.

"James, it's Domino. He worships my kick drum."

"Okay, what about Cal? Who knows something about him?"

Cherry looked at me. Her face was wrought with concern. "I told you, James. He's in trouble."

"Do you think Robo can get through to him?" I asked.

"Not a chance," she answered. "Cal's holed up in a shit-for-walls hotel on the Sunset Strip doing the Jim Morrison routine. He's not gonna open the door for anyone in the peephole he doesn't know."

"Would he open it for you?" Sponge asked.

"What do you think?" she responded.

Mike spoke for the first time. "Let's go get him! Our first road trip!"

"I don't think I should leave," I said. "What if Domino and Headley show up and nobody's here?"

"The solution's obvious," Sponge said. "Me and Cherry will go get him."

"You guys can take my car," Mike volunteered. "After I unload my equipment. Me and James can stay here and work."

"That's a bit presumptuous of you, Mike," I said, then stopped myself. "I'm sorry," I said to him. "I'm working on myself. I used to be a control freak."

"I understand," he said. "I'm kinda like that in the studio. I was just trying to help. I'm not trying to step on any toes."

"It's cool," I said. "Sponge and Cherry, do you want to go after Cal?"

"It's the only way we're gonna reach him," Cherry said. "At least as far as I can see."

"And she shouldn't go alone," Sponge added.

"Well, it's decided then. Mike, is your car legal? We can't have it impounded over an out of date inspection sticker."

"She's no beauty queen, James, but that vehicle is roadworthy and street legal. Just like my wheelchair."

"It's settled," I said. "I'll hate to see you two go so soon after you arrived, but I trust you'll be back quickly – with our lead singer."

I raised my coffee cup and toasted, "To a safe road trip to Cal E. Fornia."

"Cheers!"

***

Sponge and Cherry left the following morning. I gave them plenty of money for gas, but not enough that they might decide to hit Vegas for a night.

As they pulled away, I thought back to the carefree days of Mellowtron's first tour. We were so happy-go-lucky. I wondered if we would ever recapture that.

I turned to Mike, and he looked at me like he'd made a big mistake.

"I can't believe I just gave my muscle car to a drug addict and a stripper to drive halfway across the country."

"Consider it an investment in your future, Mike. It will go a long way toward becoming a part of the Mellowtron team. That's a big deal, because all the members of the team are equal. Let me tell you about it as we walk. I can't neglect my health regimen."

CHAPTER NINE

The next morning, Mike and I had coffee together at the kitchen table.

"I wonder where they are," Mike said, still concerned about his vehicle.

"No telling," I answered.

It may seem odd that we were not all networked up via cell phones, but Mellowtron was never a technologically modern band. The instruments were vintage 70's stuff, as was the equipment. We had an old Winnebago, rather than a fancy modern bus. You may remember from 'Band On The Run' that I used a cell phone a couple times, but after it was destroyed by the Red Baron it was never replaced. The O'Day house had an old black Bakelite phone on the kitchen wall, and that seemed to be enough.

"I don't think I gave Sponge the phone number here," I said to Mike.

"Figures."

"Don't worry so much, Mike. Things just kinda work out with this band."

Mike thought about what he knew of Mellowtron – the 'Bago getting blown up, the bitter breakup, my supposed death – and looked seasick.

I noticed Mike turning green and offered hope. "Mike, don't feel so ill at ease. Let's just do what we can and let the pieces fall into place. Have faith and let not your heart be troubled."

As the words left my mouth, I realized I was being James Blank again, manager and... know-it-all?

"Thanks Mr. Blank," Mike said. "Things will work out, huh?" There was a note of hope in his voice.

I had taken a step forward in my re-invention. I did the

right thing, but hadn't been condescending or mean. I hadn't *always* been rude in the past, but I wanted the new manager of Mellowtron to *always* be in control of his emotions. I was proud of myself. Not arrogant hubris, mind you – maybe a better description is that I was satisfied. I had done the right thing the right way.

"Mike," I said. "I think we should occupy ourselves with good work. If we sit around, we might worry."

"I'm gonna worry, regardless, James."

"Don't!" I said. "Have faith – for without faith all you have is worry."

"Wow."

"Believe," I said.

"I do, James. I believe."

"Damn good coffee, huh?" I said.

"Inspiration to the last drop," Mike replied. "Fill it to the brim."

I poured java into his cup and smiled. "It's gonna get better, Mike. Trust me."

"I do. Tell me what we're gonna do today."

"Let's go for a walk and talk," I said.

"You can't neglect your health regimen."

"Right, my good man. Let's go."

We smiled at each other like old friends.

***

We started out from the backyard, as was my habit. I didn't traverse the same path on any of my walks, but I always ended up at the mulberry tree. The treks were meant to be explorations of the surroundings, as well as the body and the mind. The area was dotted with large plantation houses not unlike the O'Day Mansion, and the thing about plantation houses is that they have plantations behind them. There were vast tracts of land in various stages of use. Some were pastures for docile herds of cattle. Some were small parcels occupied by a testosterone-enraged bull. Some were fields of cotton. Some were soybeans. Others were wheat, peanuts, and corn.

As we walked, Mike and I discussed Mellowtron's next album. Mike assured me he could record a bootleg-quality demo with his chair that we could shop to the labels, but I informed him of the way Lucite Records had screwed the guys. We would be going it alone this time. The record would be self-released.

"So we're going to record a professional quality album with my wheelchair, James?" he asked.

"Nope. We're going to build a studio in the house. I've already decided the location. There's a small bedroom and a large bedroom next to each other on the second floor. We'll cut a hole in the wall between them and put in glass. The little bedroom will be the control room, and the big one will be the main recording studio."

"All the best classic rock albums were recorded in houses," Mike said.

"I know."

"It will be just like Headley Grange," he said.

"Let's just hope *our* Headley Grange shows up," I replied.

***

Back at the house, I retrieved a notebook and showed Mike the Mike the bedrooms I thought we should remodel.

"Looks perfect," he said as he stuck his head into the larger bedroom's huge walk-in closet. "We can turn this into an isolation room for the drums."

"There's even a bathroom," I said. I walked over to it and opened the door.

"This is a perfect vocal booth," Mike said as he walked

through the narrow door to join me inside.

"You think we should remodel the bathroom, too?" I asked.

"No way. It's perfect as it is. All this ceramic tile and porcelain will create awesome natural reverb."

"You think so?" I asked.

"Listen, James." Mike burst into song in a loud falsetto voice. "I see a little silhouetto of a man-o!" The bathroom's acoustics made his admittedly unprofessional voice as beautiful as the sound of a well-tuned Stradivarius.

I smiled broadly. "Mike, I think you're on to something!"

Mike looked at himself in the bathroom mirror and curled his lip in a Billy Idol sneer. He leaned his head back and screamed, "I LOVE ROCK AND ROLL!"

"PUT ANOTHER DOLLAR IN THE JUKEBOX, BABY!" I answered.

"It's a dime, not a dollar," he said.

"When's the last time you saw a jukebox that took dimes, Mike?"

"Good point," he said.

"That gives me an idea, Mike. I want to buy an old Wurlitzer jukebox for the lounge."

"What lounge?" he asked.

"The one we're going to build." I sat down on the edge of the bathtub and started drawing diagrams in my notebook. Mike sat down across from me on the toilet seat, not bothering to put the lid down.

An hour later, we left the bathroom with a loose plan. I knew I was overly optimistic, being that we only had one band member committed to the project – the drummer, no less – but the work would keep our minds from worrying.

After ordering a vintage Wurlitzer jukebox on eBay,

Mike and I made BLT's in the kitchen.

"What's our budget on this project?" Mike asked as he spread mayo on toast.

"Why do you ask?" I said, paranoia creeping in.

"Well, I need to know what kind of equipment we're gonna use. Are we going bargain basement, or what? I mean, the label ripped you guys off, right? I assume we're broke."

"Yeah, the label ripped the guys off," I said. I knew Lucite owed me a lot of money, since I had only signed the original contract, not the one that was re-worked to screw the members of Mellowtron out of their royalties. Lucite Records still thought I was dead, though, which complicated things. Finally, I found it simplest to say, "I came into quite a bit of money, Mike. Let's leave it at that."

"Yeah, but about the equipment," he persisted.

"Spare no expense."

"I'm still gonna buy used," Mike said. "Vintage is where it's at."

"Exactly," I agreed. "You'll record on one and a half inch tape, right?"

"I'd much prefer two inch, James. With a Mackie 48-track board. Using tube amps and effects knocked down to Pro Tools on a Mac Pro."

A surge of confidence coursed through me. This guy knew his shit.

Mike continued. "If we can't get Mellowtron together to do another album, I guess we can record other bands, right James?"

"Bite your tongue!" I scolded. "You do have a point, though."

"The studio needs a name," Mike said.

"I agree. The O'Day Mansion isn't the most rock and roll of names. We've got plenty of time to think about it.

Something will come to us."

"What do we do first, James?"

"Buy a truck. We're going to be doing demolition, and we'll need materials for the re-model. I'm sick of not having a vehicle."

Just then I heard a sound from the driveway. It wasn't the throaty V-8 of Mike's muscle car. I looked out the window and saw Domino stepping out of an old orange and white Chevy long-bed pickup. He looked as tall and skinny and confused as ever.

"Mike, answer the door for me. Domino is here – the bass player. Make up a bunch of stuff like you don't know him. Do everything you can to confuse him. I'm gonna sneak out the side door and surprise him."

"Can do," Mike said. He left and ran downstairs, then sat in his wheelchair and rolled to the front door. He answered before Domino could knock.

"Waddya want?!" he screamed. Domino jumped. "I didn't order no pizza, boy!"

"No-not-no-not pizza," Domino stammered.

"What is ya, then?!" Mike demanded.

"I don't know!" Domino answered, terrified. "Who are you?"

"I'm Mama Kin!" I was creeping stealthily around the house and had to cover my mouth to keep from laughing. "And I'm loadin' my guns, boy!" Mike acted like he was doing something with the arms of his wheelchair. "And I'm fixin' ta shoot!" Domino turned and ran back to his truck. By this time I was sitting on the passenger side of the truck's bench seat.

Domino jumped in and frantically struggled to start the truck. He looked at me and said, "James, we gotta get outta here."

"Everything's fine, Domino."

Domino shrieked as he realized he was sitting next to the ghost of James Blank. He looked at Mike on the porch, then back at me, then collapsed like a droid that has just had its power supply removed. He didn't faint like Sponge. He just shut down from the overload. I've seen goats do the same thing on the internet.

Mike walked up to the truck's driver-side window and looked at Domino, who was now snoring. "Is this guy okay?" he asked.

"I'm sure he's fine," I said as I got out of the vehicle. "He's tougher than he appears. Looks like we got that pickup, huh?"

"Yep. It will make a fine work truck. How long are you gonna let this guy sleep?"

"I'm gonna make him some french fries. They're his favorite. It will help minimize the trauma."

"Nothing surprises me around here," Mike said.

"Get used to it."

I whipped up some homemade pomme frites in the kitchen and walked them out to the pickup. I reached in and held the steaming plate an inch below Domino's nose. He woke up quick, like I had used smelling salts (or one of Sponge's socks) on him.

Domino looked at me, nearly in tears. "James, are you real? Please be real. Are those fries real?"

"It's really me, Domino. I'm sorry I left you."

"I don't care about that, James. I just want you to be real." He took the platter of fries from me and set it on the seat next to him. He reached and grabbed me by the neck and pulled our heads together in the truck's open window.

"Are you really real, James?" he asked.

"I'm really real, Domino. And I'm real sorry."

Domino let out a wailing sound, which could have easily been interpreted as despair, but I knew it was joy.

A squeal of tires and the throaty growl of a well-tuned V-8 engine came from the end of the driveway. I pulled away from Domino's grasp and looked toward the sound, expecting the General Lee, but it was Mike's Super Bee, and Cherry was at the wheel.

She executed a flawless power slide as she neared the house, and the vehicle skidded to a majestic stop. Cherry popped out of the car in a button-down white shirt, which was rolled up over her stomach and tied in a knot. She had high-waisted white shorts on and white go-go boots. She was channeling Pinky Tuscadero, smacking gum and smiling, her auburn mane shining in the sun. The wind from the open driver's window had feathered her hair perfectly.

"Where's Sponge?" I asked her.

"Passed out in the back seat." Smack, smack.

"Did you get Cal?"

"Wadda you think? Come see for yourself."

This felt like an especially cheesy episode of 'Happy Days'. Thank God, Potsie Weber and Ralph Malph had long ago been executed with a single bullet to the back of the head by Mr. C. after they violated Joanie Cunningham behind Al's Drive-In, or they probably would have driven up next.

As I approached Cherry, she walked around the car and popped the trunk. I walked up and looked inside and saw Cal curled up with Crisco, both asleep.

I was speechless. I looked at Cherry, then at Cal and Crisco. My lower lip quivered, and I said, "God bless you, Cherry!"

I reached into the trunk and shook Cal, then Crisco, but they did not move.

"Oh no," Mike said from behind me. "The exhaust leaks into the trunk. They're dead."

Cal and Crisco remained motionless, and it didn't look like they were breathing. Thoughts of soul-crushing loss and failure rushed into my brain. This was going to be the end of everything any of us had ever tried to do. Period.

"Crisco! Cal!" I reached in the trunk and shook them violently, but there was no sign of life.

Sponge woke up in the backseat and climbed out of the car and staggered up to me. "James, who are you?" His eyes were crossed.

"Leaks into the backseat, too," Mike said.

"Walk him around!" I ordered, ushering Sponge toward Mike. "Get some oxygen in his lungs!" I turned back to Crisco and Cal. Mike put his arm around Sponge's waist and led him away.

"God, please don't let them be dead," I mumbled in an awkward attempt at prayer.

God must not have had much going on that day, because Crisco opened his eyes. He couldn't focus – he looked like the canine version of Ray Charles sans glasses. He recognized my voice, though, and his tail wagged slowly.

I grabbed Crisco and lifted him from the vehicle and carried him over to the elevated porch where I laid him down softly between two of the columns. "Nurse, give him mouth to nose!"

Cherry didn't object in the least. She calmly walked over and stooped down and planted her lips directly on Crisco's cold nose and blew like she was inflating a pool float. After doing so, she pressed against the dog's ribs to cause him to exhale, then repeated.

I hustled back to the car and reached in to pull Cal out. His legs were moving, jerking apart from one another. "He's trying to do a scissor kick!" I said. I yanked him out of the trunk and onto his back on the grass.

I looked over and saw that Crisco had been revived and was now laying on his side with his head up. He looked at me with a dazed expression.

"Cal's turn, Nurse Cherry!" I said. I walked over to Crisco and fell against him, pushing my face into his side. Cherry rushed over to administer her life-saving skills to Cal.

I hugged Crisco, then pulled back to get a good look at my former friend. "God I love you, you crazy mutt!" I said. "Where have you been all my life?"

Crisco looked at me and smiled, now nearly conscious. "Rowwrrr," he said softly, wishing he could speak human. He laid his head back down.

"Rowwrrr back at ya," I said. "You're gonna be okay, boy."

I looked over at Cherry, who was blowing air into Cal's nose. If it wouldn't have been a matter of life and death, I would have laughed. Cal came to, choking and sneezing. I noticed he had gained a considerable amount of weight, but was wearing a pink spandex unitard, regardless. It was not a good look. He looked like an undercooked and overstuffed bratwurst.

We helped Sponge and Cal to the porch and sat them down in lounge chairs. Domino walked over without aid, but was still trembling from the shock of his scare. Crisco stumbled over and laid down on his side. He was drifting in and out with his long tongue hanging out the side of his mouth. I walked to a place in front of everyone and spoke two very important words. "We're back."

Sponge and Cal said nothing. Their eyes were rolling around in their heads, and their tongues were hanging out similar to Crisco's. Domino's head was swiveling around frantically, scouting for ether bats and seagulls.

"You guys look worse than that morning in Vegas," I said. "Too bad the studio isn't complete. You look like you're ready to record your next hit."

"What about Headley?" Mike asked.

"That *is* a problem," I said. "I can't for the life of me think where he might be. He should have been here by now if Robo had located him."

"Take to the internet!" Mike said.

"Tally-ho," I replied. "Nurse Cherry, will you sit with our new arrivals? They need more fresh air."

"I'll monitor them, Dr. Blank."

I smiled, basking in the latest addition to the many titles I once held. "Follow me!" I said to Mike the Mike.

We walked in the house to the entertainment room, and the phone rang. "Go ahead, Mike," I said. "I probably need to answer that. It could be Headley."

I hustled to the kitchen and picked up the receiver, hoping it was my guitar player.

"Hello," I said.

"Mr. Yames, it is Robo."

"Robo! I'm so happy to hear from you! Where are you?"

"I have the bad news, Mr. Yames. So sorry."

"Nonsense. What is it? You're doing a great job."

"I am not to find the Headley Grange. I cannot."

"Well, come home then, Robo. We'll track him down somehow."

"Mr. Yames, is it okay I do not come to you? I am in the San Francisco. I met a guy."

I was speechless, my mouth agape.

"Mr. Yames?"

"Yes, Robo. I – I'm happy for you. Will you at least

come visit me sometime?"

"That I will do to you, Mr. Yames. You know I do love you."

"Likewise," I said. "And what about your share of the money?"

"Yust hold onto it, Yames. This guy – he helps to run a company called an Apple. He has the money."

"Okay, Robo," I said with a smile. "I sure am gonna miss you. Come back and cook the Devil's Dingus for me when you get a chance."

"For you that I will cook once again. I love you, Mr. Yames. Do not be too much of the choleric!"

"I won't, Robo. I'll talk to you soon. Take care of yourself. You can keep the Taser."

"I hope you will find mister Headley Grange," he said before hanging up.

Another chapter of my life had ended. Well, maybe just a sub-chapter. Either way, Robo had served me well, and he taught me a lot about what it means to do something without expecting anything in return. My little Robo was a saint.

I went to the entertainment room and found Mike sitting in front of the computer. He had been eavesdropping, and he looked like he was feeling sad for me.

"Cheer up, Mike!" I said. "The kids are alright. We've got three quarters of the band here. Let's put on a pot of java and do some research on Mr. Headley Grange."

CHAPTER TEN

Morning came quickly. Mike and I hadn't left the computer when the sun came up. Nurse Cherry had long ago transported her patients to bedrooms of their own to recuperate, and all were sleeping peacefully. The old house served well as a makeshift hospital ward, but it needed to undergo a transformation if Mellowtron was ever going to get out of intensive care.

The night's research on Headley had yielded few clues. He seemed to have dropped off the face of the earth. All our internet searching came up with were things created by fans – live videos of his solos and top ten lists. He was well respected. His name appeared next to other virtuoso guitarists like Eddie Van Halen and Jimmy Page, but nothing indicated any sightings of him in the last couple years.

Though we had worked through the night without sleep, I was unwilling to call an end to our search. I went to the kitchen and made a fresh pot of strong coffee and brought it to the entertainment room.

I noticed Mike had about fifteen windows open on the computer and was clicking through them with purpose. "James, I can't tell when these videos took place," he said as I sat down next to him. "He plays the same guitar in every video. Everybody else plays different guitars as their career progresses – it functions as a timeline. I've got no chronological specificity here."

"Headley only owns one electric guitar. He modeled it after Brian May's."

"Hmmm. Brian May, huh? One other thing, James. Take a look at this." He clicked on one of the windows, and it opened, displaying a page with dozens of pictures of people's right hand. The pinky finger was missing from each of them.

"What the hell is this?" I asked.

"Look at the title of the website, James."

It read 'The Headley Grangian Society' in bold letters.

"The Headley Grangians?" I said. "Oh my God!"

"People are cutting their pinky fingers off to honor Headley."

"I see that, Mike. Unbelievable."

Just then, I felt incredibly tired. I excused myself and suggested we retire, but Mike said he was going to keep researching. I went to my bedroom and saw Crisco splayed across my bed. Of course.

I shoved him to the opposite side and slipped under the covers. I petted Crisco's head a few times and appreciated that he was no longer a greaseball, then fell asleep.

Crisco and I slept through the day into the next night, switching sleeping positions numerous times. At one point I woke to find his dog butt inches from my face, but simply turned over, exhausted. Nurse Cherry popped in from time to time to check on us. I woke around two in the morning and went downstairs. My biorhythms were way out of whack. Crisco did not follow.

The house was silent except for the muffled sleep-sounds emanating from various bedrooms. I saw a glow in the entertainment room and went to it and found Mike still at the computer.

"James Blank!" he said as I entered the room. He had seen my reflection in the monitor.

"Mike the Mike. Have you been up this whole time?"

"Pretty much. I might have dozed off for a few minutes, but I found him, James. I'm sure of it."

"Found who?"

"Headley! He's with Brian May."

"Mike," I said. "I think it's time to get some sleep."

"It's true, James. He's studying astrophysics. Brian May is teaching him."

"Mike, you really need some sleep. You're hallucinating."

Mike whipped around and glared at me with flaming, computer-fatigued eyes. "It's true!" he hissed.

Now, I have been around all manner of tokers and tweakers on epic benders, but this dude looked ravaged beyond anything I'd witnessed. He exhibited psychotic symptoms worse than a computer geek who's been on a three day 'Call of Duty' bender.

"It's all about GRAVITY!" he screamed before launching into hysterical laughter. "I can see up Saturn's Uranus!" Then he made a sound like a cheap firework lifting off from the pavement. "Vvvvvvvvvvvvttttt!"

"Cherry!" I screamed.

Nurse Cherry appeared at the entrance to the room. "What is it, doctor?"

"Nurse, this man needs Niacin. Vitamin B-3! Nicotinic acid! STAT!"

"Roll out the B-3!" Mike shouted. "Hammond, you idiots! Ham and rye! Ham and cheese! Ham and organ! Velveeta, Goddamit!! Bring me some queso fresco and the head of Alfredo Garcia, if you don't mind."

Cherry rushed away and returned with a large, brown bottle. "The vitamins, Dr. Blank."

I took the jar and emptied the dozen or so pills into my hand, then slammed them down on the coffee table. I used the empty bottle to crush them into a mix of powder and jagged, meteor-like chunks, pieces flying everywhere. "Get me a straw, Cherry!"

She left again and came back quickly and handed me something I hadn't seen since about 1980. It was a crazy straw, made of hard plastic. "It's the only one I could find," she said, her eyes desperate.

"It'll have to do." I handed the straw to Mike and ordered him to snort the vitamins. He inhaled forcefully, but could not propel the crumbs through the curly-cues. The straw was clear, and I could see that the medicine had clogged in the first loop-de-loop.

"Dammit!" I said. Mike was huffing and puffing and sniffing and snuffing and getting nowhere. "Lean back!" I ordered.

Mike the Mike tilted his head back, still holding the straw to his nose like a confused cokehead. I put my mouth on the butt end of the plastic pipeline and blew as hard as I could. Mike shuddered as the crushed vitamins entered his system, then collapsed on the couch. I watched him for a minute, sure that he would launch into a fit of convulsions.

"Shall we carry him to his room?" Cherry asked.

"He looks comfortable to me, nurse," I said. "Let's go back to bed."

"But doctor..."

"That's not what I meant, Cherry. Go back to sleep. I'll be in the sack with Crisco."

"Yes, your honor."

***

I slept the rest of the night and through most of the next day and woke in the early evening, my biorhythms still screwed up. Neglecting my health regimen hadn't helped, so I took Crisco for a long walk. I talked to him along the way. He was older now, probably middle-aged in dog years. His temperament had mellowed. When we reached the mulberry tree, I sat down for a break.

"Crisco, I sure missed you, boy." I said. "Sit down here by me." Crisco laid down next to me and rested his head on my thigh.

"I'm sorry I left you," I said as I stared out at the point where the horizon meets the sky.

"I can't explain why I did what I did. Everything just came crashing down when I found out the old debutante was dying. Just like when my mother killed herself."

Tears trickled down my cheeks as I finally found the answer I had been searching for with all my self-analysis. The old debutante had taken the place of my mother. When she passed away, it was like my mother dying all over again.

"The bell tolls for thee, you old bitch," I said with a half-smile. It felt as if a baby hippo had been lifted from my shoulders. I sat up straighter with my back against the old tree. The sun was in the last stages of setting, and it was brighter than a welding torch. I stared into this vast, ageless nuclear orb – the rock star of the Milky Way – for long seconds before closing my eyes, sure that I had been blinded by the light.

The sun set quickly, but its memory still burned brightly on the inside of my eyelids like an image melted into the screen of an old computer monitor. I opened my eyes and attempted to focus on the zenith point just above the now obscured sun. The night was awakening around me. The temperature dropped quickly. The summer was turning into fall. I sensed all this – my blind gaze did not leave that spot above the horizon. Slowly, my vision returned, and another light show was just beginning. The Leonid Meteor shower was in full bloom – my burning bush. God was speaking to me. I smiled. Without drugs, I had achieved nirvana. The word means 'blowing out', and my brain was doing just that – through the top of my head. I was commuting through hyperspace in a VW van with the Dalai Lama. Jerry Garcia was along for the ride, too, and all of us were blissed to the max.

Out of the deep blue, Crisco ladled my face with a long, moist slurp, which interrupted my vision. He was standing in front of me with his front paws on my shoulders and his back legs standing on my thighs. I turned my head to the side, but Crisco licked my cheek as hard and fast as he could – ruff love.

I was back in the now, now – no longer transcendentally medicating. I laughed and grabbed Crisco and hugged him. "Let's get home, boy!" I cradled his head in my hands and kissed him between the eyes over and over.

We set out for the O'Day Mansion together in the clear night. The stars flickered above us, resembling Chinese lanterns, and the glowing meteors descended like dying fireworks.

Nearing the house, I detected an orange glow. I smelled the familiar scent of roasting wienies and toasted marshmallows. Crisco was hungry and broke into a sprint. I heard a roar of happy exclamations and laughter as he met the group. A minute later, I strolled up to the friends I had been away from for so long. They had built a large fire inside the brick boundary of the old, dried-up fountain.

"James!" they said as a group. I looked at them – all together again, except for Headley. Their faces were bright and rosy in the firelight.

I raised my hands to silence them. They hushed, and I spoke.

"My brothers, I have missed you more than you can know. It's time for us to do the great things we were supposed to do, but never did. I'm sure that's why we've been brought here. I'm different now. Are you? I've been dead on my feet for two long years, but now I have risen. Have you done the same?"

The group gave a half-hearted affirmation, somewhat bewildered by my strange words.

I continued, "Are you guys alive? Alive enough to help those that are dying? Do you feel strong? Strong enough to help those that are weak? Will you listen to those without a voice? Will you fix those that are broken? If you have a home, will you offer shelter to those in need?"

They cheered and yelled out.

"Yes, James!" said Domino.

"Hell, yeah!" added Sponge.

"I am so strong!" Cal proclaimed.

They were behind me as usual, but I had never had a problem pumping them up. They were practically begging to be led, but this time I wasn't giving them a pep talk before a gig – this was a pep talk before the rest of our lives.

I scanned them and asked a final question. "Do you believe in love?"

There was no response for a moment – they were silently contemplating if they were honestly capable of perfect love.

Crisco broke the glassy silence with a howl, and everyone cheered and laughed.

When they quieted, I asked again, "Really, guys. Do you believe in love?"

"I believe," said Domino.

"Me too, James," said Sponge.

"Me and Cherry believe in love!" Mike said, eyeing Cherry hopefully.

"What about you, Cal?" I asked.

"I can learn to love again," he responded.

***

We sat around the campfire for hours, watching the shooting stars and talking. I suggested we discuss the future and what we wanted to accomplish with the rest of our lives. I was sowing the seeds of love and optimism, fomenting growth and development. I was being the new James Blank.

"I just want to be together again," Domino said. "The whole group like we used to be."

"Yeah," Sponge said. "I love the 'Loaves and Fishes', but I want us to go it alone this time. Plus, I'm sober now and having them around would threaten that."

"And Da Dirty Third Warders are dead," Domino said.

"What happened?!" I asked, alarmed.

"A satellite fell on their tour bus," answered Domino.

"A satellite?"

"Yeah. It re-entered earth's atmosphere and landed right on top of them. NASA said it was gonna land in the ocean."

"It didn't," Sponge said.

"Tragic," said Cal. "Now, who the hell are these 'Third Warders'?"

"Are you guys telling me that a freakin' spacecraft landed on their tour bus – just like the Red Baron landed on the Sopwith Camel?" I asked incredulously, remembering White Folks' exhortations to the heavens after the disaster in Galveston. "Bow your heads in prayer," I said without a pause.

I did my best approximation of a prayer/eulogy, highlighting the features and benefits of White Folks and his rapper friends.

When I finished, we all said "Amen" together, and Cal said, "Who are these third-world people?"

"Let's turn in," I said, not wanting to put the spotlight on Cal's mental deficiencies. "We're all tired."

"I'm not," said Domino. "Cal, you don't remember Da Dirty Third Warders? We spent the last half of our tour with them."

"I'm sorry, man. I can't remember anything. I remember you guys, but that's it."

"Do you remember what you call your penis?" asked Sponge.

"PeeWee?" Cal answered hopefully.

"That's your dog's name," I said.

"Poodle!" Cal said with a stupid smile on his face.

"Poodle what?" asked Sponge.

"That's what I call my penis!"

"Not quite, Cal," I said. "Looks like everyone knows what you call your penis except you."

"I don't know what he calls the bloody thing," said Mike the Mike. Cherry whispered in his ear. "Really?" he said.

I spoke firmly. I didn't want Cal's tenuous grip on sanity threatened. "Guys, it's time to turn in. We're off to a good start – a step in the right direction. I'll wake you in the morning, we'll have breakfast, and we'll get started on a brand new day."

***

The next morning I let the boys sleep late, but I piped in some subliminal music to usher them into consciousness. I put the kitchen stereo in front of the intercom and scotch-taped down the 'TALK' button, then pressed 'PLAY' on the little CD player Robo had left behind. The disc spun and 'Would' by Alice In Chains started. I had selected the 'Singles' Soundtrack, but I quickly re-thought my choice and skipped to the second song, 'Breath' by Pearl Jam. I wanted to re-instill joy in my boys, and if there's been a band in the post-classic rock era who can blast a bit of joy, it's P.J. I hit 'REPEAT' on the player and got back to my cooking.

The song resonated softly through the house, 'breathing' life into rested bodies. I percolated coffee and fried bacon, their aromas providing the best wake-up call of all.

One by one, the occupants of the O'Day Mansion drifted into the kitchen. Small talk was made, but we had known each other long enough to give a little space in the morning.

I walked to the stereo and forwarded the CD to 'Chloe Dancer' and pushed 'REPEAT' again. Twenty minutes of the song would do us all good. I had a theory I was putting into practice with the music I was selecting. We had all been adrift, unconnected. Music had taken a back seat. I hoped to pull us back together with great songs. I wanted all of us to be singing the same song in our heads at the same time.

Finally, I served breakfast, and we ate in satisfied silence. I was no mind-reader, but I had a strong feeling that everyone was thinking about my words from the previous night, Cherry and Mike included.

When the meal was finished, I spoke. "Okay everyone, put your dishes next to the sink. I'll wash them today, but from here on we'll share the chores. Is that okay with everybody?"

They nodded agreement, so I said, "You've got ten minutes to make a phone call, smoke a fag, or go to the restroom, then meet me in the backyard at the fire pit."

The appointment was met, and I looked at each of my comrades, interpreting what I could of their demeanor.

"Is everyone happy?"

Nobody spoke.

"Are you confused?"

The band members muttered in the affirmative and looked awkward. They were dressed in their street clothes in the bright sun and getting a little uncomfortable.

"I haven't been outdoors this much in the last five years," said Sponge.

"Just as I suspected," I said. "You've neglected your

health regimen. Nurse Cherry?"

"Yes, your honor doctor."

"Are you ready?"

"Never more so."

"Okay, men. Nurse Cherry is going to be so kind as to take you on a fast-paced nature walk. Enjoy your surroundings – and your thoughts. Meditate."

"Tally-ho!" I said, and Cherry was off. Cal, Domino, and Sponge stood in front of me, not moving.

"Guys, look," I said as I pointed at Cherry, who was walking away quickly in her pink hot pants and hiking boots. "Look!"

"Got it, James," said Sponge as he rushed to catch up with her. Cal and Domino came to their senses quickly and did the same. I laughed at Domino's tight black jeans, knowing what he was in for.

"Don't forget to take a break at the mulberry tree, Cherry!" I called out. She gave me a 'thumbs up' sign with her left hand without turning.

"Wow," Mike said. "You're doing it. I can really see it. You're rebuilding this thing."

"Let's hope so," I said. "Are you ready to get to work?"

"The studio?"

"Not yet. I've got another project for you. Don't worry – it's right up your alley."

***

Back inside the house, I explained to Mike what I wanted – good speakers throughout the house. The little intercom wasn't cutting it. "I want the whole house linked up," I said. "If I play something on the computer in the entertainment room, I want it to be broadcast all over."

"And the control room in the studio should be tied in, too, right, so we can listen to the mixes?"

"Exactly."

"But we don't have the wire or the speakers," Mike said.

"You better get online and order what you need, then. Have everything shipped overnight. I've deposited a substantial amount of money in my Paypal account. I'll give you the payment information. I'm delegating this project to you, Mike. Are you comfortable with that?"

"Sounds like my dream come true, James. I'll map out the wiring diagrams, order the supplies, then start drilling the necessary holes."

"That's my boy," I said. "I'm gonna work on getting Headley back."

"About that," Mike said. "I'm ashamed of how I acted the other night."

"Let not your heart be troubled, my friend. We all have our moments."

"I was expecting a guilt trip."

"Guilt trips aren't worth the time it takes to book the reservations, Mike. And you were right – Domino gave me Headley's big sister's phone number, and she assured me that Headley is, indeed, with Brian May. I'm gonna work on reaching him. You better get started hard-wiring the house for hi-fi."

"You got it!" Mike rushed off, needing no more direction.

I sensed movement at the top of the stairs and saw Crisco descending slowly. He was stretching every step or two, doing canine yoga poses.

I looked up at him, and he caught my glance. "You gonna help me do the dishes, or what? There's no garbage disposal, so I need the plates licked clean before I wash them." Crisco barked happily and hurried down the stairs and followed me into the kitchen.

***

After completing the chore, I made dozens of calls, then sent out a handful of emails. This was looking to be one of the most frustrating and difficult tasks in my managerial career. I was attempting to reach Brian May, one of the biggest, and most private, rock stars on the planet. On top of that, he had been famous for over forty years. He was entrenched and surrounded by seasoned 'gatekeepers'. Gatekeepers are the term I use for the people that guard celebrities. Gatekeepers are very similar to politicians – they may start out good, but are inevitably turned bad due to their access to power. As the old saying says, "Power corrupts, and absolute power..." – you know the rest.

I got frustrated and gave up. I had done all I could for the time being. Just then, Cherry popped into the house and stood before me, running in place. "Your boys are outta shape," she said.

"Where are they?"

"They collapsed in the backyard."

"I'm gonna have a group session with the guys, Cherry. Do you want to sit in and document it?"

"Will you give me fifteen minutes to shower up?"

"Of course. We'll be waiting for you out back."

***

I walked around the house and found the three members of my band in matching piles of agony.

"How'd it go, guys?" I asked.

"My God, where did you get that chick, James?" asked Sponge. "She's a dominatrix."

"Oh pshaw," I said. "She's harmless."

"You go on a run with her, then," said Cal, who was on his hands and knees. He looked at me with a defeated expression and said, "That chick is a she-Nazi."

"The Nazi's didn't get in shape doing Zumba," I said.

When I uttered the word 'Zumba', Cal's expression went full retard. His eyes wandered independently of one another, and he fell over in a lump.

Domino crawled over and helped me examine our lead singer.

"What happened?" he asked.

"I have no idea, Domino. When I said 'Zumba', something short-circuited in his head."

"You know that's what he calls his penis," Domino scolded. "How could you do that? He's in a very delicate state."

Domino laid Cal on his back on the grass and gave him the once-over, then looked earnestly at me. "James, Cal should be in the butterfly ward at a mental hospital. His sanity is touch-and-go – mostly go."

"I understand, and I'll keep that in consideration. I'm gonna try to work with him first. I was worse than him, and I came back."

Sponge spoke in a stern voice from a few feet away. He was in a bad mood as the result of the strenuous exercise. "There's a lot of nonsense going on around here. I still trust you, James, and I'll give you a second chance, but this whole reunion is hanging by a spider web."

"That's the strongest thing in nature," I replied with confidence.

"I'm back, boys!" said Cherry as she strode up with a bounce in her step. The guys groaned.

"Not again," Sponge said.

"No more running for today," I answered. "Your health regimen has been satisfied and not neglected. Now we must work on our minds. Gather round. Sit Indian-style on the grass." Mike strolled up, pushing his wheelchair, and I told him to join us.

There was some grumbling, but my instructions were followed. When we were all seated, I reached behind me and pulled something from my waistband. I held it up triumphantly. "This is one of John Bonham's drumsticks. It was used at a concert in Sacramento in 1977."

"I taped that show!" said Mike the Mike.

"How did you get that stick?" asked Sponge.

"I bought it on Ebay."

"Probably fake," Domino said.

"It's absolutely real. Notice the embossed signature of Bonzo, himself. Do not doubt the spirit of Led Zeppelin, or you'll end up melted like a Nazi in an Indiana Jones movie. We're going to talk, one at a time. Get things off your chest, and say what needs to be said. But the only one who can talk is the one holding this sacred drumstick."

I handed it to Cal.

After a long pause, he seemed to regain consciousness and spoke in a Tarzan-like clipped voice. "I was once powerful. I cast spells over the people." He waved the stick like a scepter. "I was a golden god." He handed the talisman to Sponge sitting next to him.

"What am I supposed to talk about, James?" he asked.

I shrugged my shoulders. I didn't have the stick, so I had suddenly been stricken mute.

"When James died everything went to shit," Sponge said. He handed the stick to me.

"You guys think I betrayed you," I said. "I understand that, and I'm sorry. I offer no excuses, but you need to know something. My mother killed herself. Her arms were wrapped around me when the life went out of her, and I couldn't do a thing. I was just a small child. When the old debutante passed away, it was as if my mother died a second time. I was powerless, and I couldn't handle it."

Domino held out his hand for the stick, and I passed it to him. Our eyes locked in a sincere gaze. "James, that is all the explanation I need. I forgive you and ask your forgiveness in turn."

I nodded back at him. I didn't need to speak.

"When the band broke up," he continued, "I was completely lost. I listened to people that didn't have my best interests at heart. They told me to record a solo album and play all the instruments myself. I'm a bass player, dammit, and that's it! Who would have thought I could pull that off? I'm not McCartney, for God's sakes!"

The rest of us didn't speak, but offered low, "Um-hmms." We understood and shared his pain.

"I couldn't write shit," he said. "I was desperate. I tried to re-create 'Back To The Water'. I was still scared of seagulls, so I laid down in a field with a bunch of rotten meat. Vultures landed all over me. It was an absolute nightmare, but it sure as hell didn't inspire any music. Then I tried to contact you with a Ouija board, James, but you kept hanging up on me."

Sponge reached to Domino and took the stick from him. "I pissed away everything I had. I got one decent royalty check. I thought I would be getting them for the rest of my life, but that was the only one! I blew it on skunk-weed and sushi and sake. I was so broke – my identity got stolen, and it *raised* my credit score." He handed the drumstick to Cal.

"I don't even know what we're doing," said Cal. "That's how messed up I am." He passed the baton to Cherry. She looked at me with questioning eyes. I nodded, granting permission for her to share.

Cherry held the stick in front of her with both hands and spoke to it like it was a person. "I wanna kill Boobnanza.

That bitch has ruled my life long enough! Stupid slut!" I was the only one who knew of Cherry's alter-ego. Everybody else thought she was talking about an actual person. "From now on, I'm me and nobody else!" Cherry grasped the stick like a knife and plunged it over and over into the ground.

I jumped up, afraid she would break the valuable drumstick. "There, there, girl. Give me the weapon."

Cherry bent forward and collapsed, emotionally exhausted. I whispered in her ear, and she went upstairs to her room to cry herself to sleep.

"When's my turn?" asked Mike the Mike.

I handed him the stick, which was now caked with moist dirt. He tapped it against his wheelchair sitting beside him to dislodge some of it.

"Guys, you gotta pull yourselves together. I know you don't know me, but I'm gonna speak to you as a fan. I loved you guys, 'cause you were different than all this crap coming out now. You were raw, like Sabbath when they first came out – or Ratt. I'm not comparing you to those bands musically – I'm talking about the edge you had. You were hungry. You've got to get that back. And from what I've seen of James, he's just the guy you want in your corner."

I reached to Mike for the stick. "Thanks, Mike. These guys need to remember what they're capable of doing, but let's not blow smoke up each other's asses. We have all fallen to what I sincerely hope is the low point of our lives. We're like those Chilean miners. We're down in a hole, and it's time to dig ourselves out. We're missing Headley – he's fallen down a well somewhere, too, I'm sure, but he'll be back someday."

"I've thought a lot about our past," I continued. "We didn't have a long-term plan. I should have had a better strategy. We got lucky, but it came too fast. Success fell in our lap, but we didn't know how to handle it. This time it's going to be different. We control our destiny, and it starts tomorrow."

"It starts right now!" yelled Domino. "Oooowwwwoooooo." He beat his chest like an ape, which caused him to start coughing.

"Let's start rehearsing in the morning," said Sponge.

"Hold on, guys," I said. "We can't rush this. We can't start rehearsing tomorrow. We need to start building the recording studio tomorrow. Make sure your intercoms are turned up, and I'll wake you in the morning. Goodnight!"

I walked away with Crisco, and Domino said, "James Blank has left the building."

***

I woke early in a happy mood. I showered and went downstairs, giving the stair lift the finger as I pranced down the steps without aid. I put on some music and piped it into the intercom. I started with a mellow song – Jackson Browne's 'Cocaine'. It sounded like a vintage Stones acoustic tune, and I thought it might inspire some last minute dreams of sobriety and non-neglected health regimens.

I had Little Smokies sizzling by the end of the song. Coffee was beginning to percolate. Still, nobody had entered the kitchen. I played 'Men of Good Fortune' by Lou Reed while I cracked eggs onto the electric griddle. It would have been a great song for them to rise and shine to, but nobody stirred.

Breakfast was nearly prepared by now, and I was using all my newly-found coping skills to remain composed. I picked up another CD and smiled. "This should do the trick," I said.

I put the disc in and turned the volume up and pressed 'PLAY' and turned back to my work. As the first bars of

Megadeth's 'Wake Up Dead' pummeled the house, I nodded my head to the beat, smiling.

Mike the Mike was the first to push open the swinging door to the kitchen.

"Morning, Mike," I said without looking. "I hope you slept well."

"Slept great," he replied. "Crazy dreams, though."

At that instant I had a wonderful idea – I filed it in the 3"x5" recipe card file in my head under the heading, 'Ideas, Implanted'.

I walked to the stereo and turned the volume down. "Did the Megadeth song wake you up, Mike?" I asked.

"I guess, but I could barely hear it over that old intercom system."

"So you don't think it's going to wake the others?"

"Not unless they're light sleepers."

"They most definitely are not," I said. "Will you please go wake them? Breakfast is almost ready."

"It's the least I can do. I appreciate you putting on such a nice spread."

"Don't worry, Mike. You'll make it up to me. I've got lots of work for you."

"Can't wait to hear about it," Mike said as he pushed the door open and walked out.

Fifteen minutes later, the gang had assembled in the kitchen and filled their plates. The little table only accommodated four people, so Sponge and I stood and ate at the counter. When we were finished, I addressed my friends.

"Are you guys ready to get to work?"

Everyone answered in the affirmative.

"What about our health regimen?" Cherry asked. The guys groaned.

"We'll get back to that, Cherry, I promise, but it's going

to be less important as we move forward. We'll be getting plenty of exercise working on our projects."

"What projects?" said Sponge.

"I'm glad you asked. Let's meet in the formal dining room in thirty minutes, and I'll tell you what we're gonna do. Check that – I meant to say that I'll *ask* you guys what you think about my proposals. Nothing has been decided or will be without your input." This was the new James Blank talking again.

Everyone left, and I sighed as I picked up the dirty dishes and moved them to the sink. The door swung open, and Domino stood there.

"You never took me hunting seagulls," he said.

"I don't even know how to load a gun," I replied.

"So it was all a lie – you never shot crows in Oklahoma?"

"It's a true story, but it was my grandfather. He told it to me right before my mother died. I wasn't trying to lie. I was trying to motivate you." I looked at Domino, then dropped my gaze in shame. "I'm sorry. I'm working on being a different person now. I'm trying to get better."

"What happened to your grandfather?" Domino asked.

"I'm sure he died decades ago."

"I bet he's proud – looking down on you."

"Sure. He's watching me eat crow."

"He's watching you become a grandson he can be proud of."

I looked at Domino and wanted to smile, but didn't. "You think?"

"I know. Besides, how can you eat crow if you don't even know how to shoot one, James?"

Domino had just paid me back for all the pep talks I had given him over the years. He had no conception of this, which was no surprise. I was the leader. I was the one who handed out compliments and discipline and gave pep talks. Nobody else was ever going to fill that role for Mellowtron if I had anything to do with it, and I could never expect to be told, "Good job." I didn't need that, anyway. I'm sure nobody ever walked up to Patton after a battle and said, "Nice job, General."

Domino and I washed the dishes without speaking, happy to be in each other's presence. My mind pored over battle plans and managerial strategies and executive decisions, and Domino watched the soap bubbles pop.

***

We met in the formal dining room at the agreed time, and I spoke to the group tentatively. "Guys, just let me know if you don't like my plan."

"What plan?" said Sponge.

"The plan I'm going to propose. If that's okay with you guys. Is it okay?"

"Is what okay?" asked Domino.

"I'm lost," said Cal.

"Maybe Mike the Mike should tell you," I said.

"Tell us what, James?" said Cal.

"Just tell us!" begged Domino.

"James, just tell us what to do and stop beating around the bush," said Sponge.

"But I don't want to boss you around," I said. "I don't want to be a dictator."

"You aren't a dictator, James," said Sponge. "You're our manager. Now stop being so nice and tell us what the plan is."

"The plan!" said Cal.

"We want to hear it," said Domino.

"Me, too!" added Mike the Mike.

"Yes!" said Cherry in a lusty voice. All eyes turned to her, and my plan was forgotten by all of us, even me.

CHAPTER ELEVEN

I stood in the doorway and flipped the switch to turn on the single bulb that illuminated the rickety stairway leading down to the basement. The light flickered, but stayed on to my surprise. "Follow me down, but be careful," I said. "We don't have insurance for falling down the stairs."

I led the way, wondering what I would find. It had been over a decade since I'd been down here, and it didn't look too good the last time I saw it.

We gathered at the bottom, the bulb providing just enough glow for us to huddle closely together in it, surrounded by blackness thicker than chocolate pudding. The air was musty. We were breathing 2000 air. That's not a futuristic term. The basement door hadn't been opened since the year 2000. It was beyond stagnant. It felt viscous like lumpy gravy.

"Wait here, guys," I said.

Domino spoke. "It's not like."

"We're going anywhere," finished Sponge.

"Just wait here," I said. I felt for the wall nearest me and used my hands to guide me to a spot ten feet from the group. I found the metal cover I was searching for and opened it and flipped the breaker switches to 'ON'.

Lights popped and rubber belts on electric pulleys spun to life with a familiar hum. Electricity excited the electrons of noble gases, causing neon signs to spark to a warm glow.

For an instant, we witnessed an incandescent 50's memory revived. I don't know the cause. It could have been an hallucination, or we might have been seeing ghosts – happy ghosts. Vintage teenagers populated the giant room for a frozen, fleeting moment, like a picture from Ozzy and Harriet's photo album. The ghosts paid no mind to us in their

Norman Rockwell purgatory, a level of Hell not spoken of by Dante. They drank Cokes from little bottles and smiled and laughed. Then a bright Pepsi sign, pressurized and filled with carbon dioxide and other gases, exploded, and the ghosts were gone.

It was like something out of a movie. One minute we were witnessing a glorious merry-go-round of a teenage dream, but it instantly transformed into a fossilized carousel of frozen motion and silent sound. The bowling alley had switched from vibrant to dormant, like flipping the cover of Styx 'Paradise Theater' from front to back.

"It's a bowling alley!" yelled Domino. Possibly, I was the only one who had seen the ghosts.

"Who wants some action?" asked Sponge. "Ten bucks a game." He walked quickly to the racks of balls lining the walls and fingered their hibernating holes.

"Is this 'The Plan'?" asked Mike.

"It's part of our health regimen!" said Cherry.

"Everyone wait!" I said.

Sponge froze and turned to face me. I saw from the corner of my eye that the others were looking at me, too.

"This is the studio," I said.

"What? I thought the studio was going to be on the second floor," said Mike.

"We can't record in a bowling alley," said Sponge. "That's crazy."

"Everybody just hold on," I said. "We're not going bowling, and we're not recording down here. This is what we're going to use to construct the studio – the maple planks from the lanes. It's the best kind of wood for reverb."

"Aahh," Mike said. "We're going to harvest the hardwood. That'll be perfect!"

Domino and Sponge looked at me, hurt. "This could be

fun!" Domino said. "We need a bowling alley."

"Yeah, a place to take the edge off, James," said Sponge. "We want to go bowling when we feel edgy."

Cal spoke, too. "I want to have fun. I never have any fun."

I looked at Mike, and he nodded in affirmation that I was doing the right thing, but Cherry avoided my eyes.

I hadn't expected this.

"Dammit, guys," I said. "I had a plan."

I looked at the five sets of eyes fixed on me – one set in agreement and four pairs silently pleading their case.

"I'm willing to change my plan to make you guys happy," I said.

"Yay!" said Domino. "Let's bowl!"

"Not so fast," I said. "We're gonna compromise. There's six lanes. We're going to rip up five of them and use the wood to build our studio. The sixth lane will stay – for our enjoyment and our health regimen. But you can't bowl until each day's work is done. We must be disciplined. You guys better try out the lanes, so you can pick which one to save."

My friends yelled in a happy, exuberant burst of joy, as if an American Graffiti teenager had just bowled a turkey.

It was time to start the reclamation project of deconstructing the bowling lanes. There was just one problem – we didn't have any tools.

I pulled Mike to the side for a quick chat. I hadn't known the guy for long, but I had assessed him to be honest and mature. "Mike, I haven't got any hand tools." Sponge, Cal, Domino, and Cherry were slinging balls down the lanes happily.

"Well, that's a problem, isn't it?" he said.

"Yeah. Here's the thing – I don't want the boys to sense any misstep in my planning. I'm trying to assert discipline and affirm trust."

"I understand."

"I need you to be the leader when I'm not around." I felt like a general talking to his favorite second lieutenant.

"But the guys don't even know me."

"Mike, they're natural born followers. Take the reigns, and they'll pull your sled wherever you want. Just try not to let them know you're in control, if that makes any sense."

"I think I know what you mean. You're saying use a light touch."

"Exactly. I want you to take charge right now. I'm gonna take Domino's pickup and find a lumber yard and buy tools. I've got a vision of what this house can become, but we've got to get in front of things. My planning has to be better."

"Yessir. Let's win this," he said.

"They're all yours," I replied. "Good luck."

Mike turned toward the guys, who were looking into the void where the bowling balls had gone, wondering why they hadn't come back. Cherry was sitting in a chair looking at her reflection in a glossy pink 8-pound ball.

Mike took charge like a natural leader. "Boys, huddle up at the top of the stairs. You too, Miss Cherry. Hustle!"

They raced past me, and I couldn't stifle my smile. Mike's words drifted down the stairwell as I knelt to examine the construction of the floor. "Boys, we can't neglect our health regimen. We're going for a run, and I'll have no griping. Have you ever seen a fat rock star?"

"No," they answered in unison.

"Cherry, lead us, please." I heard them traipse out the front door.

I went upstairs and outside to borrow Domino's truck. I figured the keys would be in the ignition, and they were. I drove around until I found a quaint lumber yard/hardware store. A man who introduced himself as Roy Lee came to assist me as I walked in. He was thin, wearing worn jeans and boots and a pearl-snap shirt that should have been donated to Goodwill long ago. There was nothing out of the ordinary about him, except his tooth. That sounds like he only had one tooth, but he had a mouthful, all as straight and white as anyone lucky enough to be born in America, home of the braced and retainered – all except a single Southern rebel. One of his two front teeth stuck straight out like he had tied the world's strongest dental floss around it and attempted to pull a 747 out of a ditch.

The man was helpful and well-spoken, but I couldn't look him in the face for fear I would stare at the ivory tusk parting his lips where most people would hold a toothpick. This was similar to the problem I had with buck-toothed Robo and others with hairy facial moles, goiters, or a stray booger. For the life of me, I can't keep my eyes from focusing on these abnormalities like I focused on my own zits as a teenager. This guy must have thought I was the shyest person alive, because I could not meet his glance.

"We need tools," I spoke into my chest. "All the usual hand tools – enough for a half-dozen laborers. We're reclaiming wood from an old bowling alley and building a recording studio with it. Just please gather everything you think we'll need."

"Ahh," he said. "I helped a buncha longhairs with the same type-a thing a long time ago. A studio called 'Muscle' somethin' or other."

"Muscle Shoals!" I said and looked directly at him, only to turn away quickly.

"That's right, son. Said they was eternally grateful and sent me a buncha gold reckerds. They's on display behind the counter." He pointed to them, and my eyes about popped out of my head. "I just gave them a few pointers," he said and laughed.

"May I look at the gold records more closely?" I asked.

"Sure. Feel free."

I rushed behind the counter and walked from left to right, examining each framed symbol of musical achievement. They were gold 45's, commemorating 500,000 sales of an individual single. The first was a Cher record I had never heard of, but the next two were for 'Brown Sugar' and 'Wild Horses' by the Rolling Stones. I was short of breath at this point as I continued down the lumber yard's wall of fame. The Staples Singers' 'I'll Take You There' was next, then three in a row by Paul Simon, one of which was 'Love Me Like A Rock'. My mother sang that song to me. The memory made me emotional, but I held back the tears. There were a few less consequential songs, then a number of Bob Seger tracks, ending perfectly with 'Old Time Rock and Roll'. "What an appropriate denouement to this wonderful display!" I said.

"Ain't nobody ever appreciated them gold reckerds like you, mister."

"And nobody ever will, Roy Lee. Have you ever had the feeling that something was meant to be?"

"Felt that way about Glynnis. She's my bird-dog."

"Yes, Roy Lee. That's *exactly* what I'm talking about! Now if you would, let's set up an account, so I won't have to be hauling so much cash around. I'm going to be your best customer for a while. I'll pre-pay ten thousand dollars. Let me know when that runs out."

"Dadgum, mister! Did you rob a bank?"

For a second I thought he was onto me, but I answered, "Of course not, my boy. Play your cards right, and you'll have another gold record on that wall – maybe two or three more."

"I'll help in any way I can, mister. What's your name anyways?"

"James Blank. Don't forget it."

"I won't."

"Will you provide delivery service, Roy Lee?"

"For a customer like you, I will. Let me get your information, and I'll have them hand tools to you this afternoon."

"Along with anything else you think we'll need, Roy Lee. We aren't carpenters. We can use all the advice you gave those longhairs and more."

"You have officially retained me as your construction consultant." Roy Lee smiled broadly. I felt in danger his undisciplined tooth might harpoon my eye. "Sign here, Mr. Blank, and I'll have the tools over to the O'Day house as soon as possible."

"How did you know I was at the O'Day house?" I asked, alarmed.

"That's the only bowling alley around."

I stared deeply into Roy Lee's face, snaggletooth be damned. I tried to read his mind and determine if he had any suspicions about me being at the old mansion. His face was as blank as my last name, so I smiled and said, "I'll see you this afternoon, Roy Lee."

I drove the old pickup back to the house, enjoying being behind the wheel again. My driver's license had lapsed, but I didn't care. When I got home, I found the gang lazing in the entertainment room after their fun-run, watching TV. I saw they were taking in a reality show about some slut with a big ass – Kim something or other.

"That'll be enough time wasting, everyone," I said. "Go pick out a bowling ball and meet me in the foyer."

They did as instructed and met me by the front door, somewhat confused.

"What's up, James?" asked Sponge.

"A little therapy, along with a bit of exercise."

"This health regimen is killing me," said Domino.

I noticed Cal wasn't paying attention. He was a few feet away from the group, moving strangely. I watched him for a few seconds and realized he was walking through some of his stage moves and jumps. He wasn't actually doing them, but he was tracing his way through a routine like a gymnast does when imagining a flawless run. *He's coming back*, I thought.

"Okay, guys," I said, getting back on track. "Bring your balls outside, and let's go to work." I led them to a spot just in front of the house. "You see all this overgrown vegetation behind me?"

"Yes," they said.

"It used to be a nice yard – clear it."

"How are we supposed to do that?" asked Cherry.

"I know what he means," Mike said. "Watch this." He mustered his strength and rolled his 14-pounder into the plants with a crunch.

"Who's next?" I said.

Sponge let out a laugh and threw his ball shotput-style. Domino spun around like he was throwing the hammer and launched his sideways. The ball flew an impressive distance and crashed through the back window of his pickup truck. Cal set his ball down and rushed forward and leaped into a scissor-kick. His foot and calf entered the flora and became tangled, and he landed on his back, but jumped up quickly, embarrassed.

By now the group was hooping and hollering and attempting to flatten every unwanted shrub, vine, and weed in sight. An hour later, they were exhausted. "That's enough." I said. "Go relax until further notice."

They walked away hunched and tired. "Great job, guys!" I called out after them. Just then Crisco rushed off the porch where he had been resting and ran to a spot in front of me. He stared into the newly-created gash in the vegetation and growled. I had never seen this side of him. I looked down and saw he was shaking. He barked furiously. He seemed terrified, but was willing to stand between me and danger.

I peered into the vegetation, but saw nothing. I looked at Crisco with concern and assured him that everything was okay. I started toward the house, but he did not follow. His gaze was still locked onto whatever was in the brush. I went back to him and grabbed his collar and dragged him inside.

We ate a late lunch of peanut butter and jelly sandwiches and heard a honk from out front as we were throwing away our paper plates. I looked out the kitchen window and saw a panel truck from the lumber yard backing up to the front porch between two columns. The thick porch was the perfect height for the bumper of the truck. It lined up like a loading dock is supposed to.

We walked out of the house as the man I met that morning ascended the stairs. "Howdy, James Blank!" he said.

"Hello, Roy Lee. Thanks for your speedy delivery."

"No problem." Roy Lee opened the back of the truck. I didn't see the hand tools I had requested.

"What is all this, Roy Lee?"

"It's my mobile workshop. It's what we built Muscle Shoals with."

Mike the Mike went nuts. I hadn't told him the details of my trip to the lumber yard. "Y-y-yu-you b-b-built m-m-mu-

mu-,"

"Muscle Shoals," I said.

"God bless Lynyrd Skynyrd!" Mike exclaimed. "Stick a spork in me, I've gone to Heaven!"

Roy Lee laughed and looked at me. "Guess he hearda tha joint."

"We all have," I said. "Are you aware of the place of reverence that recording studio holds in rock and roll, Roy Lee? It's a legitimate pantheon."

"I hear that it's a fine example. But it can be did better."

"How?" Mike hissed. "Tell me!"

"Don't get pushy, mister."

I intervened. "Never mind his enthusiasm, Roy Lee. He means no harm. He's just excited."

Cherry chimed in at the perfect moment. "Let me get y'all some sweet tea. Cal, Sponge and Domino – you boys sit down for a minute and talk amongst yourselves."

I ushered Roy Lee and Mike to the outdoor furniture. The band members sat on the edge of the porch with their legs hanging down. They pointed, and I saw Crisco was once again frozen in the same spot where the vegetation had been cleared.

"Guys, go check on Crisco!" I yelled.

"Now then," I said, turning to address Roy Lee. "How invested do you want to be in this process?"

"I ain't liftin' a fanger. But I'll tell y'all what ta do. No skin off my back. Long as I see somethin' in return down tha road."

In the old days, red flags would be raised in my mind – red flags with the word 'extortion' on them. "What exactly does that mean?" I said.

"Send me a postcard from Japan or somethin'."

I broke out laughing. "See, Mike? This guy's the best!"

Mike smiled. "You gonna tell us how you dunnit, mate? I'm a bit of a studio chap, meself, Roy Lee."

Mike had launched into a British accent out of nowhere. Under most circumstances, this would be an indication of multiple personality disorder. Not here – it made me smile. There's no use in pretending we didn't have a specific goal – to make music that sounded like British classic rock. British classic rock made in Alabama.

It also brought thoughts of another person close to me who had assumed a British accent – Headley Grange. "Roy Lee, can I leave you two? Will you give Mike your advice on building the recording studio? I have urgent business to attend to."

"Sure, James. I'll find you when the truck is unloaded, and you can sign the ticket."

"Mike can sign it for me, R.L.," I said.

I looked over and saw the guys crouched around Crisco. Cherry arrived with the drinks. "Thanks, Cherry," I said as I took a glass from her tray. "Mike and Roy Lee, when you decide where to set up the mobile workshop, have the guys unload the truck. I must run along. It really is urgent business." I rushed into the house.

***

I sat down in front of the computer and said a mental prayer as it booted up.

"God, wherever You are, please log me on to Headley Grange. Headley Grange, the guitarist of the band called Mellowtron, not to be confused with the house Led Zeppelin recorded their finest albums in."

What started with the most noble of intentions led to me surfing a Led Zeppelin chat site. It's hard to avoid distractions like that when you're Googling 'Headley Grange'. All clues led to Led Zeppelin minutiae and the inevitable fan comments and arguments dragged along like ugly luggage. I wasn't intending to waste time, but found myself combing through comments in a thread – *'Headley Grange or The Rolling Stones Mobile. Which was the better recording studio?'*

I was surfing around the discussion when a little window appeared on my monitor with a cute popping sound like a bubble-wrap capsule being squeezed.

'James, is that you?'

Me: 'Who is this?'

'Who do you think it is?'

Me: 'Are you a mousy former girlfriend of Headley Grange?'

'Good one, James. Where are you?'

Me: 'I'm in Stringtown, Alabama.'

'That's close to Muscle Shoals. I'll see you soon. Get ready. Bye.'

The cute little popping sound happened again, and it was over as fast as it had occurred – if anything had actually happened.

I walked out to the porch and saw that a workshop had been assembled on the opposite side of the deck chairs. It was cobbled together, but looked fit for the job – kind of like an operating room on M*A*S*H. There were band saws and drill presses and workbenches with clamps and vises. Nobody acknowledged my presence – they were all hard at work setting up the shop and deep in concentration.

"Looks good, everyone!" I said loudly. "Please stop for a moment and listen to what I have to say!"

The work halted, and my associates walked to points near me and leaned against this or sat on that and listened.

"Well, this is it, guys," I said. "Headley is on his way. Feel free to celebrate. Tonight is yours, but tomorrow is mine. Enjoy the hell out of this evening and be ready to work your asses off tomorrow. That is all."

"MELLOOOWWWWTROOONNNN!" Cal yelled.

"We're back!" screamed Domino.

"We are indeed back," I said and went in the house to take a nap. I undressed and put on my pajamas without thinking and got in bed. "We're back. Thank you, God," I whispered as I drifted off. I smiled. I slept as if my bed was floating on a gentle sea.

***

The next morning I had a short meeting with everyone in the office on the second floor. Cherry took excellent notes. I first stated that the office we were meeting in was to be the 'war room' during the completion of our multiple projects.

"Mike, are you certain as to how to proceed with the building of the recording studio?" I asked. "Did you get enough information from Roy Lee?"

"I have the confidence to move forward with the construction. I may need to consult him again in the future."

"What needs to be done first?"

"I need two of the guys to work on removing the maple slats from the bowling alley lanes, and I need one person helping me on the second floor."

"Any volunteers?" I asked.

"Sponge and me will work downstairs," Domino said.

"Looks like it's you and me, Cal," Mike said.

Cal smiled meekly. "What's your name again?"

"Mike."

"I'm just kidding. Let's do it, bro." Cal said.

"That's settled then," I said. "Cherry, what's next on the agenda?"

She lifted the top page on her clipboard and looked at the paper on which she had taken the pre-meeting notes I dictated. "It says to talk about stuff we need."

"Right," I said. "Thank you. Guys, I'm going to leave a notebook on the coffee table here. I want you to write down anything you want or need. I don't care if it's a CD, a new instrument, or a specific flavor of Hot Pocket. Write it down, and I'll look at it. If it's something I can swing, it'll happen. I'm serious – if you want a Stradivarius for a certain track, write it down, and I'll get you the closest thing."

"I pawned my bass," Domino said.

"What kind do you want?" I asked.

"I'd like a vintage P Bass, but they're expensive."

"Write it down and consider it done, Domino. Do you need a Jazz Bass while we're at it?"

Domino smiled like a kid at 3:30 on the last day of school. "What about the money, James?"

"Don't worry about what things cost," I said. "Leave that to me. That goes for all of you. It's time to make your dreams come true. All I ask in return is for you to give it all you've got, whether it's building the studio, writing the new album, or recording the songs."

"Can we get to work on that studio now, James?" asked Cal.

"Hands in," I said. "Dream Weaver on three. One. Two. Three."

"DREAM WEAVER!"

The men rushed off, enthusiastic to start their work, but Cherry didn't move. She looked dejected.

"What's the matter, kid?" I asked.

"I wanna be part of the team." She looked up at me with pouting lips. This wasn't the typical brainless hottie. She wanted responsibility.

"You're a part of the team," I said. "A very important part."

"C'mon, James. Anyone can take notes. I want to do something important."

"Okay, how about you be in charge of all the purchasing? I'll go over the items in the notebook with you, and you'll order the items I approve."

"Okay, but can I get a piano?"

"Sure. We'll definitely need one to record with. Do you play?"

"I used to take lessons."

"That's marvelous! We've never had a dedicated keyboard player. I want you to order a Fender Rhodes electric piano, too, and start practicing as soon as possible. A female keyboard player could be the perfect addition to Mellowtron 2.0."

Cherry giggled happily. "I'm going shopping on Ebay right now."

"You'll need the password."

"What is it?" she said, looking around warily.

I motioned for her to come closer, so I could whisper in her ear. "Go do some research and write down the details of the best deals," I said. "I'll give you the financial information when I okay the first purchase."

"You got it, doctor," she said and kissed me on the forehead. I felt like I had been shot with the bolt gun from 'No Country For Old Men'. I fell back onto the couch, and Cherry was gone. I closed my eyes and saw her memory on the inside of my eyelids.

I passed out. I didn't know if I was asleep and dreaming or having some sort of drug flashback. It must have been the latter, because I found myself driving the Sopwith Camel and pretend deejaying like I used to. That was one powerful kiss.

"I've been exiled on Main Street long enough, my

urchins. But it's official – I'm out of exile, and the song I play for you is 'Be Yourself'. It's all that you can do, and it's the perfect song for all you audioslaves."

"What's that, you ask? How am I not dead? Wasn't James Blank burned under a Joshua Tree? Fear not, for I have never died, not once. The song is 'Let It Bleed'. Enjoy."

This went on for another hour until I started to snap out of it. If you've ever had surgery and woken from anesthesia, you may understand the process I went through while emerging from my acid flashback. In my mind, I was speaking as smooth as cognac in a crystal glass, punching buttons and twisting dials in my deejay dream. In reality, my mouth was gurbling and darbling, and my hands were soft-shelled lobster claws. I was a freakin' Sleestak.

Consciousness finally hit like a brick through a snowman's head. I made a face like I was smelling roadkill, disgusted with myself as I came to. I looked down at my body and saw Brundlefly. I very nearly erupted from each of my orifices.

I looked around and saw that I was alone, thank God. I laughed nervously and looked at my hands again. My thumbs clicked against my fingers quickly like greedy pincers. I was still drifting in and out.

"You're losing it, champ," I said to myself. I stumbled downstairs and heard hammering from the basement as I staggered to the porch to get some fresh air. I turned right as I crossed the threshold and fell into a wicker chair, gasping for oxygen and understanding of what had just happened to me.

Precious sobriety finally pumped through my veins. I thanked the God of my understanding and gazed across the front yard, the sun's warmth welcome on my cheeks.

I saw Crisco, once again frozen at the edge of the

uncleared part of the yard. I felt normal now. The sudden intoxication of the flashback had been terrifying after two years of abstinence.

I gathered my faculties and walked over to my dog. I wanted to get to the bottom of what was bothering my four-legged friend. I felt sorry for Crisco. He had always been so happy-go-lucky, but now something was making him miserable.

"What's wrong, boy?" I asked as I crouched next to him and petted his head.

He didn't look at me, but kept his worried gaze on the spot in the brush. He let out a worried whine.

"Is there something in the bushes?" I asked.

He glanced at me quickly with a furrowed brow and then at the vegetation and then back at me. He was frustrated and nervous to the max.

I stared into the overgrowth, searching for a bigfoot or an Alabama Yeti or whatever was bothering him so much. At first I saw nothing, but on my second pass I saw a pair of yellow eyes.

"It's just a raccoon, Crisco. Go scare it off."

Crisco didn't move. He looked up at me and shook his head 'no'. He was terrified.

"Oh, c'mon," I said. I tossed a pebble to scare the animal away, but it didn't move. I waded in and pushed the branches aside to get a clear look. "It's a dog, Crisco. She's scared."

Crisco stood up and did a quick circle and sat back down and let out a deep moan.

"What are you so scared of, Crisco? It's just a dog. C'mon girl. Show yourself."

The dog slinked out of the brush with its head down. She circled quickly a few times, then laid down on her side and lifted her back leg slightly, exposing her belly. I crouched next to her and petted her head and rubbed her stomach.

"She's nice, Crisco. She's shy."

Crisco was beside himself, beyond agitated.

"You're jealous," I said to him. "Don't worry, boy. You'll always be the number one mutt in our camp."

I turned to examine the new dog more closely. She was as big as a wolf and had thick black fur, which was sleek and clean. Her eyes were the color of amber resin, with black vertical slits like a cat's. She wore no collar, but had a piece of thin metal across the front of her neck. It looked ancient, like a bronze artifact. I examined it and saw that it had a hole on each side with fur threaded through and knotted to keep it in place. A word had been stamped into the metal – 'Akeldama'.

"Ak-el-da-ma," I enunciated. "That's a weird name for a dog." As I spoke the word, Crisco shot off toward the house.

"What's the deal, boy?" I called after him. "She can be your girlfriend!"

Akeldama looked up at me with pleading eyes. "Do you need some food, girl?" I asked. She nodded her head slowly as if she understood what I was saying. "Well, come in the house."

My acid flashback was forgotten, but it had planted the seed of an idea in my barren, but fertile brain.

CHAPTER TWELVE

A week later, much progress had been made. The maple slats from the basement had been removed and stacked to prevent warping and were now being affixed to the walls and floor of the budding studio. Mike the Mike had been invaluable, running wire nearly twenty-four hours a day. Daily shipments arrived. Instruments and equipment and other supplies were being shipped to the lumber yard and delivered by Roy Lee, who was profiting nicely from the arrangement. Mike the Mike took the opportunity to pick Roy Lee's brain each time a truckload was unloaded by the boys. Cherry was holed up in a room on the second floor with a newly purchased vertical grand antique piano with ivory keys, looking down on the decayed, but majestic, backyard as she played along with Fiona Apple and Tori Amos CD's.

I hijacked Mike the Mike for a day and had him finish stringing wire throughout the house, and speakers were now live in every room. I explored and claimed a room on the long-ago abandoned third floor of the mansion as my deejay booth. The third floor was primarily for storage, not unlike an attic, but it had a single small room built over the top of the porch. The little room had an A-frame construction, with a peak in the center and a ceiling that sloped down steeply on each side. A large window allowed a marvelous view of the lush green below and the blue sky above. It had been a fortunate discovery through enchanted serendipity, and I was intent on realizing my acid flashback dream of broadcasting my own internet radio station.

Akeldama insinuated herself into the Mellowtron family easily, to the alarm of Crisco, who then spent most of his time under the house – he crawled into the building's crawlspace through the ripped-out bowling lanes. As much as we coaxed and called, he would not come out, so we set bowls of food down for him, which he dragged into the darkness to consume and pushed back to the original spot after he had licked them clean.

None of us had time to speculate on what was bothering Crisco, other than the obvious fact that there was another dog on his turf. A very large one, at that.

***

Another week passed, but things did not go at all well. Every step forward was met with dozens in the opposite direction, and it seemed we were being sabotaged. One morning we woke to find the blossoming studio flooded with water. Somehow, the bathtub faucet in the restroom/vocal booth had turned on in the middle of the night, even though nobody would admit to using it. The plug was in the tub, though, so we knew somebody had consciously overfilled it. The day was lost, our time spent mopping up water and removing sections of the floor.

A few days later, an electric skillet in the kitchen turned on in the middle of the afternoon while everyone was hard at work. Bacon fat had been left in it after breakfast, and it ignited in a grease fire, nearly burning up the kitchen and the house and the studio and all our future plans.

In the case of both disasters, Crisco found me and led me to them in the nick of time. Without him, the house would have been damaged significantly or even destroyed.

The night after the kitchen fire I had a nightmare that terrified me. I dreamed that Crisco was caught in a steel trap somewhere by the mulberry tree. He could not cry out – his snout was wrapped in a barbed-wire muzzle. Dreams being what they are, I could somehow see him, but I didn't know where he was. It was terrifyingly sad. He was helpless, waiting to die or be found, whichever came first. I searched frantically, but I could never find him, so I guess the second option happened, at least in my dream.

I woke in despair – there's nothing worse than a helpless animal or child being abused. I sprang to action, dressed, and ran to the basement. I jumped into the void left by the removal of lane five of the bowling alley. I crawled on my hands and knees, frantic and unaware of the spiders that jumped off their webs onto me as I passed. I called for Crisco, but he did not respond.

I couldn't see a thing. I looked back at the light streaming through the hole behind me and crawled back to it as fast as I could, then climbed out and hustled to the cabinet under the kitchen sink to retrieve a flashlight. I found one and checked that it worked and ran back downstairs and into the hole.

I saw a flash of animal eyes as I swept the beam of light around wildly. Crisco was in the farthest corner, in the darkest and most difficult to reach spot. I low-crawled over and embraced him. He was caked with dirt and whining in despair. He licked my face, but it wasn't his usual boisterous kiss. It was like a wounded soldier in a foxhole, saying, "Climb in here, American. It's safe."

"C'mon, boy, let's get out of here." I nudged him, and he clicked his teeth at me and dug in to resist.

"Okay, Crisco. We'll just stay here, then." I relaxed and curled up next to my forlorn terrier. I rested my head on his side and fell asleep with one of his front paws in my hand.

Hours later, the sound of calls from Mike and Cherry and the band woke me. There was a new voice among them, which I recognized. It almost sounded British. Almost.

"Headley's home, Crisco!" I said. "C'mon, boy. Let's get out of this foxhole."

Crisco forgot his fear for the moment, and we crawled to the light in the old bowling alley. When we got to the hole, I picked up my favorite dog and tossed him through the portal and followed.

"Headley!" I wailed. "Headley Grange! Where the hell are you?!"

I raced up the stairs behind Crisco, who was barking maniacally.

As I passed through the doorway at the top of the steps I saw him. He looked to have been traveling for some time. An acoustic guitar without a case was slung across his back. He was dressed like a British lord, with dark brown corduroy, soft white cotton, and touches of oiled leather in his clothing. He was bearded, and his hair had grown very long – both had streaks of gray. He looked to have aged significantly, but in a very graceful, British way.

"James Blank," he said as he saw me. I stopped and smiled as I sized him up, fighting back tears. I had become so emotional lately. "I'm so bloody glad you're alive, mate," he said, as if I'd just washed up on his desert island. He extended his right hand to shake mine. I looked down to grip Headley's hand and saw his pinky was gone.

"God, it's good to hear that sorry British accent," I said with a smile as we exchanged a firm handshake. Crisco barked happily, and Headley bent to pet him and let the dog lick his face.

"We're all back where we're supposed to be," I said as I moved to hug my friend. Sponge, Cal, and Domino joined us. After a long moment of reunified, reunited, requited love, we stepped back to give our guitar player some space.

Headley looked at his band mates, now circled around him. "I hope you blokes haven't thought I abandoned you."

"We all abandoned each other," Domino said.

"God, I'm glad you're back," said Sponge.

"Please don't call me that. Just call me Headley like you used to. Even Clapton couldn't live up to that."

Cal and Domino looked at me, confused.

"I'm joking!" said Headley, and we all laughed.

"Time for a jam session," Mike said. "I'm gonna record it with my wheelchair!"

"I'm so excited!" Cherry exclaimed. "Mellowtron is reunited!"

"And it feels so good!" sang Cal. A muddy look came across his face. He had no idea why he had blurted that out, but I smiled, hoping synapse junctions were healing themselves in the maze of his memory.

"Shall we meet in the backyard in an hour?" I said. "Crisco and I need a bath first."

"I'll build a fire in the fountain," said Mike. "And load my wheelchair."

***

I carried Crisco up the stairs. He was filthy, but so was I. I didn't want to put him down before I got to my bedroom, for fear he would run back down into the crawlspace. When we got to the room, I closed the door with the back of my arm and laid him down at the foot of my bed. "Stay here, boy. I'll run a nice, warm bath for you."

I went to my private bathroom and prepared a bubble-bath for my matted and dirty friend. I came back to the room, but did not see Crisco. I didn't call for him, but lifted the bed-skirt to look under the bed.

"Crisco, will you please come out? Nothing's gonna hurt you. I promise." Crisco low-crawled to me. "Get in the bath, boy," I said. He rushed to the bathroom and jumped in the tub with a splash.

I spent the next half-hour massaging suds into Crisco's

coat and and absentmindedly talking. Lately, whenever I spent time with him, I drifted off into contemplative introspection. It relaxed both of us, though.

I lifted Crisco out of the tub and attacked him with fluffy towels, one in each hand. "Are you happy, boy?" I asked after I'd finished drying him. Crisco nodded his head. He understood most things I said to him. He was one smart mutt. I went to the window and saw that a fire had been lit in the backyard fountain/fire-pit, and hot dogs were being roasted. Domino had a metal rake with wienies stuck on each prong, cooking a dozen at a time. *Same old Domino*, I thought.

I turned back to my dog. "Crisco, I know the weight of the world is on your furry little shoulders, but can you have fun tonight – like old times?" Crisco looked at me and smiled and jerked his head toward the bedroom door, eager to go downstairs. He pranced like a reindeer on a roof.

"That's my boy," I said. "Go get a wienie!"

Crisco didn't move, but motioned for me to go first – the little gentleman, as always. He walked slightly behind me down the stairs, out the front door, and around to the backyard.

As we strolled up to the backyard jamboree, Crisco saw Akeldama, who was being fed a toasted marshmallow by Sponge. With a barrage of barking, Crisco sprinted at the black bitch and hit her in the side with his chest at full speed, which sent them both rolling in a biting ball of canine rage.

Crisco was less than half Akeldama's size, but he was blind with rage, and we were too scared of being bitten to try to separate the animals. There was only one thing that could inspire this sort of manic fury – fear. And one other thing – a guardian protecting his family. It wasn't jealousy, like I had initially thought.

After interminable, helpless seconds, Akeldama retreated into the trees with her tail between her legs. Crisco gathered himself and walked slowly back toward our group. He was wary and worried that he would be scolded. He stopped ten feet away, looking depressed and dejected.

"Crisco, you're just as much a part of this band as any of us," said Sponge. "I mean, you're responsible for the kick drum sound."

Crisco raised his head and looked at us with eyes that spoke volumes – volumes of abandonment. He did not want to be a stray again. He did not want to be given away like he was to us.

"Crisco, we're soulmates," I said. "I don't know what happened to you when I left, but I'll never leave you again. I promise."

"We love Crisco," said Cal as a memory came back to him. It was almost a question, but not quite.

Crisco smiled and barked two times. He was happy. He rushed up to Headley and jumped up on him, which nearly knocked the pencil-thin guitarist down.

"So this is the new Mellowtron," Headley said as he petted Crisco. "Supposedly dead manager, James Blank, is some sort of zombie who sleeps in the crawlspace of an old mansion with his formerly sweet terrier, now a devil-dog."

Crisco barked sharply, nodding his head wildly and smiling.

"What have you got yourself into, Headley?" asked Cherry, looking coy.

"And who might you be?" asked Headley. He had seen the girl, but had ignored her, acting aloof.

"I'm your new keyboard player. My name's Cherry Topping."

The four original members of the band looked at me

with a lot of confusion and a little anger.

"We'll see about that," I said. "There have been no promises made."

"It could definitely work," said Cal. "A hot guy and a hot girl on the same stage."

"With a virtuoso guitarist," Headley said.

"And a ragged, yet hypnotic drummer," added Sponge.

"And me," said Domino. "Seagull killer."

"If we all believe in love and love each other, the sky's the limit," I said. In the old days I would have said something stupid about me being the best manager in the world, but these were not the old days.

"I'm set to pop, here," said Mike, fiddling with the last minute tweaks of his wheelchair.

"There's no pressure, guys," I said. "Let's eat and talk, and if you want to jam after that, you can. Everything has to come naturally. Don't get discouraged if it doesn't happen."

"Either way, I'm set to pop," Mike said.

Headley looked worried, and I could see he was questioning his decision to come to Stringtown, Alabama.

"Grab a wienie and have a seat, Headley. I'll try to get you up to speed," I said.

I once again explained my disappearance – this time giving a quick background on the tragic relationship with my mother and the role the old debutante had played in my life. Then I told Headley about the two years I had spent in debilitating solitude with my manservant, Robo. I had grown weary of telling the story, but when I looked up after recounting it yet again, everyone was in rapt attention with car-crash expressions on their faces.

"I'm better now," I said, which broke the malaise. "Why don't you tell us what you've been up to, Headley."

"Well, I made a pilgrimage to my Mecca."

"Great Britain," I said in unison with Sponge and Domino.

"Exactly. Of course – Great Britain. I didn't know where I was going, though. I landed at Heathrow and rented an open car and lit out for the countryside. I spent a day driving aimlessly until I stumbled upon a special place."

"Headley Grange," I said. "That's the place you found."

"Right-o, James. Something drew me there, like Devil's Tower in 'Close Encounters'. It reeled me right in."

"What happened when you got there?" asked Domino. "Did you find Jimmy Page."

"No. I found God."

"Eric Clapton?" asked Sponge.

"It's true," said Headley, ignoring Sponge. "Like I said, this was my Mecca. My Decca, too," he laughed. "I laid down on the lawn, and The Spirit washed over me. I was one with the universe. Then I went to a pub and happened to sit down next to Brian May."

"Sounds like it's a small world over there," Mike the Mike said.

"You wouldn't believe," said Headley.

"Well, what happened?" asked Cal. He hadn't recognized the name of Jimmy Page, but the mention of Brian May had sparked something in his scarred cerebellum.

"I bought him a pint of Guinness. Then we talked and talked. Actually, he talked, and I listened. He's a very passionate man. We arranged to meet the next day for lunch and go for an outing after that."

"An outing?" I asked.

"Yes. Brian May is now a passionate advocate for animal rights. We went out in the country to disrupt an illegal fox hunt. We ran into the countryside on foot with hunting horns, which we used to disorient the hounds and warn the foxes. Brian had the physical stamina of a thoroughbred. We were very nearly shot by a terrier-man."

"Unbelievable," I said.

"Believe it. From then on, we were inseparable. He taught me astronomy and astrophysics."

"Did he teach you anything about music?" asked Domino.

"Not a note. He's retired from that, basically. He might play the occasional award show with Lady Gaga, but all he really cares about now is animals."

"Which explains why he played with Gaga," Sponge said.

"So how long were you with him?" asked Mike.

"A year and a half. He said I was ready to enroll at Oxford for a Ph.D. in astrophysics. That's when I crashed into my old friend, James, at a speed of one megabyte per second."

"Was anyone hurt in the wreck?" asked Cal.

"Surprisingly, no," Headley said with a slight smile. "It was all virtual. Nothing like the car crash I had in front of that music store years ago."

"I never got the bill for that accident," said Sponge.

"It's just like it went up in smoke," said Headley.

"Freakin' Pinto," replied Sponge with a chuckle.

***

We finished eating, and the boys seated themselves around the fire to make an attempt at playing music. I recognized something right away – they were nervous. In the old days, any number of substances would have been abused by now to numb each of us in our own idiosyncratic way. Now, we were all stone-cold sober. I didn't say anything about it, hoping it would work itself out. I knew if the music would just start, we would be transported to nirvana, and it would be Strawberry Fields Forever – but that was a big 'if'.

"Okay, what song do you guys wanna play first?" asked Domino. "Glue Room?"

"I don't remember the words," said Cal.

"How 'bout 'Tequila', then?" said Sponge.

"I can't remember that, either," said Cal.

"It doesn't have lyrics, Cal," said Domino. "It just says 'tequila'."

"How am I supposed to remember that?" Cal asked on the verge of panic.

"I'm set to pop here, guys," said Mike.

"Hold it! Everyone stop," I interrupted. "I warned you guys that this wasn't going to come easy. Nothing valuable ever does. Try not to get frustrated. We've been away from this for a long time, but Mellowtron *will* continue, mark my words. I don't care if we play Christmas carols, but we need to find something we all know – to unify us. Got any ideas, Headley?"

Headley strummed a few chords on his acoustic guitar absentmindedly while he thought.

"Wait," said Sponge. "I need a drum. Do we have one, James?"

"No. You haven't placed your order in the notebook, have you?"

"I kinda forgot."

"We'll have to improvise," I said. "I'll be right back. Everyone think positive thoughts for a minute." I went to the house and returned with two phone books and handed them to Sponge. "The thick one is Birmingham. It's the kick drum. Play it with your hand. The Mobile phone book is the snare. You can play it with the John Bonham stick, but be careful." I handed the drumstick to him gingerly.

"Cherry," I said. "We'll be ordering a number of things

in the morning, starting with drums."

"Yes, your highness."

I looked to see if Cherry was being sarcastic, but she was sincere as ever, which made me smile slightly. "Headley?" I said. "Did you come up with a song?"

Headley's scarred hands sprang to life, inspired. He was the only one who had maintained his musical chops, despite the loss of an appendage. The thin fingers of his left hand fretted some simple chords while he finger-picked a beautiful melody on his old Martin western-style guitar. He resembled Jimmy Page in his prime – concentrating intensely, but looking like he had almost forgotten he had a guitar in his hands. I smiled as I recognized the song. After sixteen free-time bars, Sponge whacked on the Mobile phone book with John Bonham's former drumstick.

Thwack! Thwack!

"On a dark desert highway," we sang together. Cal looked around, confused. He didn't even recognize 'Hotel California'! He had once been a scholar of all things classic rock, but the drugs had obviously taken a toll.

I whispered to Cherry to run in and print out the lyrics for Cal. She smiled at me with genuine warmth and ran to the house. Our affection for one another was sincerely familial – she was like my niece, and I was like her crazy uncle.

Crisco circled the perimeter of our group as we sang, watching for Akeldama's yellow eyes in the trees.

"Here you go, James," whispered Cherry when she returned.

I motioned for her to give the paper to Cal, and she looked back at me, uneasy. I motioned again. She walked over and handed the lyric sheet to him like she was asking for his autograph. Cal pulled a Sharpie from inside his spandex tights, but realized what he was holding just before he wrote his signature. He pulled the marker back and looked slightly confused. Cherry tip-toed back to where she was sitting.

"Welcome to the Hotel Alabama!" Cal belted out. We all looked at each other in amazement and smiled. His tortured larynx had more soul than ever. Being down on the upside on the Sunset Strip had added depth to his instrument.

Inspired by the voice we had all been so in love with years ago, the song did not want to end. It went on for a half-hour, devolving (or evolving) into rounds, like how 'Row Your Boat' is sung. Finally, it descended into soft finger-picked guitar strings, and Cal almost whispered the final words. We were all mesmerized.

When the song finally stopped, there was silence for long seconds. Then Mike, Domino, Sponge, Cherry, and I yelled out, "YEAH!" It scared Cal and Headley – they were still in the deep trance great performers succumb to when they give great performances.

Tears streamed down Cherry's cheeks. She looked at me and said, "James, I'm the luckiest girl in the world!"

I looked at Mike. I didn't have to speak. He knew what my eyes were asking.

"Don't worry. I got it," he said as the right side of his mouth curled into a Billy Idol sneer. "I always do."

"What's the next song, guys?" I asked.

"How 'bout some Stones?" said Sponge. "Whaddya know, Headley?"

"I know every Rolling Stones song. 'Waiting On A Friend'," he mumbled, still recovering from his artistic trance-state.

"Run and print the lyrics, Cherry," I whispered.

We made the very tiniest of small talk – we were almost

speechless from the previous performance and nobody wanted to disturb the vibe. Our resident redhead returned and handed the lyric printout to Cal.

The guitarist strummed his six-string softly, and we listened to Cal and Headley work out their differences through the song, just as Mick and Keef had once done. Sponge played his phone books softly with his eyes closed.

When the song was done, I spoke, drained of emotion. "Guys, I can't take any more of this tonight. Crisco and I are going to bed. Cherry has the notebook – tell her what instruments and amps you want, and I'll order them in the morning. I'm exhausted. Until tomorrow, sleep tight for me. C'mon, Crisco."

I wasn't tired. This was yet another managerial technique, based upon the maxim, 'When the cat's away, the mice will play'. I was the patriarch of the group – the adult in the room, as it is sometimes referred to. When I left, it allowed the guys to relax, which was what they needed to do. It gave them the opportunity to catch up and get to know each other again. It wouldn't take long, since they had once been closer than brothers. I wanted them to get comfortable with Cherry and Mike, too, and vice-versa.

Crisco and I went up to my private deejay booth on the third floor, which was taking shape nicely. Within a few days, the final shipments would be delivered, and I would be broadcasting world-wide – my disk jockey dream come true.

I sat down in the driver's seat – the same model I had knocked down so many mile markers in driving the Sopwith Camel. I looked up at the overgrown visor bolted to the low ceiling and flipped it down. I swiveled the microphone stand that was zip-tied to the visor to a spot near my nose. It was just like the setup on the first Sopwith Camel. I laughed and spun the steering wheel in front of me. It wasn't attached to a steering column, so it spun around fast and smooth like a toddler's toy.

I looked at the console to the right of me. The compartments had been built into it from my memory of the Camel, and a vacant space on top waited for the laptop that would be my master controller for the whole operation. AM airwaves would be replaced by a high-speed internet connection in due time.

I gazed out the massive window in front of me, a close approximation of the Winnebago's windshield, and smiled. "Soon," I said. I caught a glint of yellow animal eyes in the uncleared brush in the front yard below, but ignored them, hoping it was a raccoon. I stood up to go downstairs to my bedroom. "C'mon, Crisco. Let's turn in."

***

The following morning I woke and went downstairs. I fixed coffee and sat in the kitchen to drink it. I decided to pump some easy listening music into the brains of everyone sleeping in. The old intercom was now a memory, having been replaced with the networked speaker system by Mike the Mike. I put on David Gilmour's 'On An Island' album. I set the volume to just above inaudible. I didn't want to wake the guys. I wanted to subliminally influence them, in reference to the 3"x5" card in my head labeled "Implanted Thoughts, Subliminal".

Crisco was laying with his belly on the floor and his legs straight back like a frog. He sure seemed a lot happier.

Something scratched at the kitchen's exterior door. I opened it slowly and saw that Akeldama had returned. Crisco popped to his feet and growled. The fur down the middle of his back stood at attention. Akeldama slinked through the kitchen and into the main part of the house. I didn't see her the rest of the day.

Crisco stopped growling when the black dog was gone, but he sure wasn't going to relax like he had before she came back.

Cherry waltzed into the kitchen and greeted me enthusiastically. She was loving her new life, having left Boobnanza in a ditch somewhere.

"How's the practicing coming along?" I asked.

"Very well, I think. I can play all of Fiona Apple's songs and a lot of Tori Amos."

"That's great! Have you worked on anybody else's music?"

"No. Should I?"

"Not necessarily. It sounds like you got your chops back, but Mellowtron doesn't play music like Tori and Fiona."

"I guess you're right," she said, looking concerned.

"Not to worry, Cherry. We've got a ton of stuff to order today. I want you to help me with it, then I've got an album I want you to immerse yourself in. We're going to order you a Rhodes piano and some vintage synthesizers. I don't want you to play until we get them. Just listen to the record over and over."

"What is it?"

"The second album of 'Physical Graffiti' by Led Zeppelin.

"How many albums of 'Physical Graffiti' are there?"

"There's two, but I want you to concentrate on the second one. After you've mastered that, you'll be ready to study Mike Garson. He played improvisational jazz piano on all the best Bowie albums."

"Cool," she said. "You ready to get those keyboards ordered?"

"That I am."

CHAPTER THIRTEEN

Another two weeks passed, and the studio still wasn't complete. One disaster after another halted the project. Tools disappeared, causing the guys to accuse each other. Wires and cords were discovered frayed, and replacements had to be ordered. Headley's hands were black and blue from a multitude of accidents, and I was very concerned that he might lose a finger on his *left* hand, which would be a disaster.

Crisco returned to his previous state of anxiety and was again under the house. Nothing was going right. The guys hadn't jammed after that first time in the backyard. They weren't in the mood after putting in long days of frustrating work. Everyone was on edge.

I realized I better do something, or there was danger of someone defecting. I piped relaxing music through the house while we worked, which helped a little. I knew I needed to get the instruments in the guys' hands again very soon. They were musicians, after all, not construction workers.

In an attempt to get started rehearsing, we set up the new equipment in the bowling alley. Nothing disastrous happened loading the gear downstairs, thank God. I looked at the band as they tuned up. Cherry made a wonderful addition to Mellowtron's image sitting behind her Rhodes electric piano. She looked at me with a nervous look, and I gave her two thumbs up like Fonzie.

I saw that Headley was frustrated with something. "What's the matter, Headley?" I asked.

"I can't get my guitar strobe-tuned," he said. "There's something wrong with the magnetic dipole and Faraday's Law is not being satisfied. The fourth harmonic is all fluxed up."

We looked at Headley in bewildered amusement, but he didn't raise his head from his guitar and tuner. He really was ready for the Oxford physics program.

Finally, the band was ready to play. "Count us in, Cherry," said Sponge.

Cherry smiled and said, "One, two, three..."

"Someone stepped in dog poop," said Domino into his microphone.

Cal looked down at his high-tops. "Ewww. It's all over me. Help, James!"

***

Thirty minutes later, Mellowtron was ready for a second attempt at practicing, after mopping the floor and throwing Cal's soiled shoes into the fire pit. Sponge clicked his drum sticks four times, and the band launched into 'Mick's Lips'.

It sounded pretty good. Cherry added subtle chords and gained confidence as the song progressed. Mike was mixing the P.A. feed, as well as the monitor mix, and he was dialing it in nicely.

The song ended, and the band quickly launched into 'Technicolor Body Fluid'. Smiles abounded. *This is just what they needed*, I thought. Mellowtron was in the groove, and Mike and I swayed to the music. We glanced at each other with a smile and nodded.

Shockingly, Headley's Marshall stack, which was nearly seven feet tall, suddenly lurched forward and toppled over onto the guitarist with a thudding crash. The band stopped playing, and Mike and I rushed to lift the heavy speaker cabinets off poor Headley. Akeldama rushed away from the scene and ran up the stairs.

We uncovered Headley, who was more shaken than injured. His experience running around the British countryside with Brian May had him in better shape than in the old days. His hands had several jammed fingers, but none appeared broken. A line of blood trickled down from his left nostril.

"That dog did it!" yelled Sponge. "I saw it out of the corner of my eye! She stood up on her hind legs and pushed the stack over on top of him!"

"That's impossible!" said Mike. "That amplifier head and those speakers must weigh two hundred pounds."

"I'm tellin' you, I saw it! You saying I'm a liar?" Sponge asked.

"He's not calling you a liar," I said. "It *is* hard to imagine a dog doing something so premeditated. Are you sure Akeldama stood up and pushed the gear over on to Headley?"

"I'm positive. Remember – I don't do drugs any more! It was no accident, and it was no hallucination."

An urgent howl came from beside us, and we turned to see Crisco's head protruding from the space where lane five used to be. He looked directly at us and barked over and over.

I rushed over and pulled Crisco out of the hole. He was full of manic energy and over-stimulated. He raced to the speaker cabinets that had fallen on Headley and sniffed frantically.

"I believe Sponge," I said. "We should have trusted Crisco's instincts. He's hated that black bitch since the first time he saw her."

"I *did* see Akeldama come out of the kitchen right before the grease fire," Mike said. "I apologize, Sponge."

"No worries," answered Sponge.

"And that explains those chewed up cords," said Domino. "I thought Cal did that. Sorry, Cal."

"I thought I did it, too," said Cal with a shrug.

"We need to get that dog out of the house," said Cherry.

"We sure do," I said. "Urgently, before she can do any more damage!"

Crisco ran to the stairs and turned and barked like Lassie. Timmy wasn't down a well, but he wanted us to follow him.

"Lead us to the bitch, Crisco," I said. We raced up the stairs behind him.

Tenacious is a frequent word used to describe terriers, and Crisco embodied the term. He searched the bottom floor with his nose and detected every place Akeldama had spent any time. We found missing tools and other evidence that the black dog had been an agent saboteur.

The hunt continued through the second floor and up to the rarely-used third. We searched the storage contents to no avail, but when I opened the door to my new internet radio studio, I saw Akeldama sitting in my driver's seat, facing us. She looked back at the window, then turned her head toward me and snarled with her lips pulled back. Crisco rushed to a point between me and her and growled like never before. He was practically screaming – something between a bark and a howl.

Akeldama looked like 'The Thing' from the John Carpenter movie – like her jaws were going to unhinge and a second mouth was going to appear from inside her throat. In the movie, the alien always has to decide at the last possible moment whether to fight or flee, and Akeldama did the same. She glared at Crisco, and an unnatural sound emanated from deep in her throat, like she was attempting to spew fire at him.

I had a maple slat in my hand I had picked up when we searched the studio. I rared back and slapped it across Akeldama's nose, which stunned the animal. She shook her head and re-grouped, then leaped from the chair through the plate glass window with a dramatic crash.

We rushed forward and saw the large canine laying on the grass thirty feet below. It was like the ending of 'The Exorcist'. Shockingly, the dog rose to its feet and dragged into the brush, near the spot where I had first found her.

It was raining, and we all stood in stunned silence, trying to process what had just happened. The rain was sheeting in and threatening to damage my new radio station.

"Damn the luck," I said. "I was going to start broadcasting in the morning."

CHAPTER FOURTEEN

I woke up extra early – way before the alarm clock was set to pop. It was still dark outside, but I was far too excited to sleep. It was a week after the incident with the black dog.

I hopped out of bed and went to Crisco, who was still asleep on the floor. I crouched on my knees and gently shook him awake. He looked at me groggily – he was getting old and appreciated sleep a lot more now than in the old days. I had no idea of his age when we adopted him. I leaned over and pressed my mouth into his head near his ear.

"Today's the big day, little guy. You just lay here while I get ready. Hit the snooze button and go back to sleep. Then we're going for a ride." Crisco's eyes lit up at the 'R' word. It seems like the understanding of the phrase 'go for a ride' is embedded in the domestic canine's DNA. "Relax, boy. I won't leave you," I said. I kissed the top of his head three times quickly before going to my private lavatory.

I restrained myself from looking out the little bathroom window while the water flowing from the bathtub's spigot changed from cold to hot. I knew what was out there in front of the house, lurking like a leviathan, but I wanted to deprive myself to prolong the experience. It was just like barbecuing baby back ribs – the longer you wait, the better the taste. It could also be compared to foreplay, but that would require rubber sheets and a haz-mat crew.

I sat on the edge of the tub and had a Blu-Ray daydream, which is what happens when you drift off into right-brain territory when you are not fully awake. It was spectacular, but I couldn't remember a bit of it after I snapped back to consciousness.

The steam rising from the now scalding water had brought me back to reality. I turned the faucet off and inserted the stopper into the drain and turned the water back on. I waited for the tub to fill while I played the song 'Berlin' in my mind at exactly the speed it plays on the album – languid and ever so bittersweet. I detected the faint smell of diesel exhaust, but did not look out the window.

As I descended tentatively into the near-boiling water, I became fully awake as I eased my nether regions in. I soaked for a bit, then washed my glorious naked body, forcing myself to linger in the water longer than I wanted, to further delay my gratification. I thought of the many sponge baths on Mellowtron's first tour and enjoyed this prolonged soak. By the time I got out, the water had cooled to luke-warm, and I looked like a California Raisin. I had deprived myself long enough, so I dried off quickly, growing excited.

I dressed in a rush and descended the stairs with Crisco at my side. The house was silent except for the creaks of the brittle antiques. We exited the house, and I ordered my loveable terrier to do his business.

I cast my gaze on the busted-looking charter bus idling in front of the house. *Why the hell do buses never turn off their motor?* I wondered, but laughed when I realized I didn't care. I had assumed the coach would be state-of-the-art, but had not specifically requested that. I needed to brush up on my managerial duties. The engine seemed to be running well, so I dismissed most of my concern.

I strolled up to the bus and rapped on the door, which reminded me of the first time I met Robo. The door opened with a luxurious 'whoosh'. The driver swiveled in his chair, and we sized each other up, and both our eyes grew round like Frisbees.

"It's you!" he said.

"I can explain."

Fire burned in his eyes. He gritted his teeth. Then he

smiled slowly. "James Blank, you greasy sum-bitch. It's me, Skunk! Do you remember me?"

Of course I remembered him. I walked out of his studio with Mellowtron's master tapes after promising a fifty percent cut.

"Is it really you?" I said as I ascended the steps toward him. He stood up and held out his arms to hug me, but his body odor beat him to the punch and embraced me in a nostril-shattering wave. I extended my arms in the same manner, but stopped short and hugged myself. "My old friend, what has become of you!" I said.

Skunk looked confused and dropped his arms to his side. "I bought this bus."

"What happened to your studio?" I asked.

"That wasn't my studio. I was just the in-house producer. Mark Slinger owned it. Some wiseguys came in after you recorded there and stripped the place – said Slinger's manager owed them money."

"Nicky," I mumbled.

"That's the guy. Nicky Pepperonzi."

"Is Mark Slinger okay?" I asked.

"Sure, if you call delivering room service at the Hard Rock Hotel okay."

"Wow. Well, it's great to see you again, Skunk. Is that seat air-cushioned and water-cooled?"

"Sure is. You sound like you're speaking from experience, James."

"Hell, yeah," I said. "You don't want to wind up like the Grateful Dead's driver."

Skunk winced and said, "Ouch."

"You got that right," I said with a laugh. "Honk the horn a few times, Skunk. It's time for the guys to wake up."

"Sure thing, boss."

"There's no hard feelings, right Skunk?" I asked.

"For what? We're legends, bro! We recorded 'Mick's Lips'!"

"Yes, we did. And you did a wonderful job, Skunk."

***

The sun rose slowly, but the damp fog numbed the sunrise. The illumination from the bus headlights extended forward in specific boundaries, like exaggerated light sabers.

The residents of the house trickled out and marveled at the old bus, wondering what it meant and what was happening.

"Everyone huddle up on the porch!" I called out.

We gathered together, and I spoke. "I know I haven't told you about this, but I wanted it to be a surprise. We're going on the road!" Murmurs of objection came from the group, as concerns were raised regarding their lack of adequate rehearsal and the condition of the bus.

"Wait," I said. "Everyone relax. I know we haven't rehearsed enough, but this isn't an actual tour – we're only playing one show, but it's very important. This gig is in a place that hasn't been touched by rock and roll for at least twenty years."

"Megsigo?" said Cal.

"Nope," I said. "Not Mexico."

"Canada?" asked Headley.

"Not Canada, either," I said. "Any other guesses?"

Nobody said anything. Akeldama slunk out of the brush and into the cargo hold of the bus, but none of us saw her.

"We're going to Kansas!" I yelled.

Silence.

"We're going to Kansas, guys!" I hollered again, hoping I would somehow win them over if I repeated the phrase more enthusiastically.

Crickets chirped.

Finally, Cherry came through like a perky cheerleader. "Woo-hoo! Let's hit the road!" This brought a couple smiles from the guys.

"All aboard for Topeka!" hollered Skunk from the door of the bus.

"Hold on," I said. "We're going to be gone for a while, and you guys haven't had a chance to pack. Get your things and be ready to leave in a half hour."

"What about the equipment?" asked Mike.

"We're only taking the instruments. We're renting everything else," I answered.

They rushed off, growing more excited by the minute.

I was packed and ready for departure, so I walked to the bus. Crisco was sniffing the tires, and Skunk was off smoking his breakfast, so I stepped onto the motor coach alone. I was humming 'One Man Band' by Roger Daltrey and had 'The World According To Garp' tucked under my arm as I sat down in an aisle seat on the front row. I got comfortable and opened the book.

"I was wondering when youse would show up."

I raised my head and looked forward to a point a thousand yards in front of me. My pupils dilated, then pinned, then regulated, all within a few seconds.

"Am I dreaming?" I said. "Or is that the voice of Nicky Pepperonzi?"

"It sure as hell ain't Mork from Ork."

I stood up and turned to see my old friend sitting in the back row. He had lost weight, but otherwise had not changed. He stood up and stepped into the aisle.

"You told the guys I was dead," I said, standing in the aisle at the front of the bus.

"What would youse have done if you were in my

shoes?" he replied.

"Were you trying to gain absolute control over them?" I asked.

"James, I thought youse knew me better than that. I was trying to take care of them. Youse of all people know that managing a rock band is pure instinct. I mean, there isn't a book to consult about how to handle a rock band in distress."

I reached in my back pocket and pulled out 'Band On The Run' and held it up. "There is now."

"But there wasn't then, James. Youse meant the world to all of us, me included. When youse disappeared, it sent me into a tailspin."

"All I can do at this point is tell you I'm sorry," I said.

"That's all youse have to do, James."

We rushed down the aisle to each other and embraced in a powerhug like grappling wrestlers.

"I couldn't let the boys think youse had abandoned them," Nicky said, still holding me.

"Say no more," I said. "I was told the mob had you on the run."

"They did for a while, but things changed," Nicky said as he released me. "I've got so much dirt on those bastards, they thought twice. They shot me a couple times, though. Helped me lose a few pounds. Fuggedaboudit."

The members of Mellowtron boarded the bus and saw me re-uniting with Nicky and couldn't believe their eyes. They thought it had all been planned. Nicky and I quickly fell into our previous roles of authority, and things were at once just as they always were.

After everyone found their seats, I spoke.

"Well, it looks like we're all where we're supposed to be," I said. "And I couldn't be happier. I want you to know that I love all of you like family – more than family, actually.

And can you believe we're going on the road again? It seems like just yesterday we were rolling around in a beat-up old Winnebago. I know this bus isn't fancy, but that's not what we're about, anyway. Let's make the best of the tight quarters, like the black groups did in the fifties and sixties when they used to tour the South in buses like this one, working the 'Chitlin' Circuit'. We'll get to know each other again."

The boys smiled, and I continued. "Guys, I don't want you to worry about this gig. I mean, it's really important, but it won't matter if you make a mistake or two. There won't be any record labels. We're going to Kansas to spread the gospel of rock and roll."

"And one last thing before we leave – don't doubt yourselves. Together we are mighty, and when we get momentum, we're like a lead zeppelin. You are gifted and very much blessed, you princes of Alabama, you kings of California, you rock stars of the universe!"

At this, the bus erupted in a volcano of optimistic cheers.

Skunk rushed onto the bus and asked, "What did I miss?"

"You didn't miss a thing, Skunk!" I said. "Let's roll!"

***

This trip turned out to be much different from our old style of touring. There were no drugs – not even any alcohol. We weren't to the point of having twelve-step meetings, but it seemed that our lives were more full than ever, even without addictive 'enhancements'. The guys didn't sleep the whole time, either, like before. It was a blast. We played games like 'Charades' and 'Name That Tune', but the most laughs were had when we got so bored we invented something completely new.

We spent hours playing a game we made up, called 'That's A Nice Dog'. Crisco was the star. He sat in a seat next to the aisle, smiling happily, as we took turns saying, "That's a nice dog you got there." The object of the game was to say the phrase in a different voice or accent than anyone else had done. We used every accent from Italian to Korean and every imitation from Christopher Walken to Mr. Magoo. I've never laughed so hard in my life. By the big smile on Crisco's face, it looked like he was laughing just as much.

When we weren't playing goofy games, the guys and Cherry rehearsed. Like the rest of our activities, this took place in a new, refreshing way, and was a marvel to behold. It was done acapella. Music can be practiced mentally, even guitar or piano. It's an amazing thing. We had a discussion about that, so the band decided to try a mental practice session. It morphed into Sponge beating on the seats for drums, with the others either whistling, humming, or singing their parts. And it was beautiful.

Mike the Mike recorded everything Mellowtron hummed or played. Nicky and I sat in the back row and got re-acquainted while the band tightened up their songs. Nicky petted Crisco's soft head while he spoke – they had really missed each other. We discussed our present situation and made a gentleman's agreement that the old cocktail napkin contract we signed years ago was valid enough to continue with – if the wheels didn't fall off Mellowtron 2.0. He told me his brother, Rocco, was managing the Loaves and Fishes, and that they were very successful.

"Are you and Rocco on speaking terms?" I asked.

"Of course. We're like brothers."

"I want you to make a call," I said.

After our conversation, I went back to observing the guys as they practiced with Cherry. She was playing imaginary electric piano on the back of a seat and singing her backup vocal parts and seemed to be fitting in nicely. The group stopped when someone got lost or made a mistake, and Cherry made her fair share. What I noticed, though, was how the guys were talking to her. She was an equal. She was into the music, and they respected and appreciated that. She wanted nothing more than to make those songs boogie, and the guys seemed to have forgotten that she was a red-headed bombshell. When hot chicks become family, they magically change from 'supermodel' to 'sister', in most cases.

I smiled and sighed and told Nicky, "I was worried about adding a chick to the band. I thought it might create internal drama like Fleetwood Mac, but I think it's going to work out."

Nicky smiled and put his arm around me. I saw a new sparkle in his mouth and noticed for the first time that he had a gold tooth he didn't have before.

"What's the story behind the bling?" I asked as I pointed to the place in my own teeth where his gold slug was.

"Don't ask, James. Fuggedaboudit. I'ma write a book someday, just like youse. Then everyone'll know the story of Nicky Pepperonzi."

"Sounds like a best-seller to me," I said. "But I didn't even know I was writing that book, Nicky. It was supposed to be my private diary."

"That Syverson asshole," Nicky said. "Want me to have his legs broken?"

"Nah. It all worked out," I said and smiled.

***

One thing I reflected on while we traveled was how I did things in the past compared to how I was doing things this time around and from here forward. In the old days, *I reacted* to events as they happened. Now, *I chose* my destiny. I had been lucky before – instinct had, for the most part, guided me in the right direction. We were successful, in spite of our addictions and dysfunctions. Looking back, I couldn't believe how lucky we had been, but it caught up with us in a big way. Someone should have dragged us into an intervention. But that's rock and roll. Just ask Steven Tyler. And Joe Perry.

***

As we pulled into the Topeka city limits, I yelled to the front of the bus, "Skunk, you know where we're going, right?"

"It's programmed into the GPS, boss. We're stopping at that schoolhouse first, right?"

"You got it."

We drove another fifteen minutes until we arrived at a very old brick building that was obviously a school. It looked like some sort of political rally was being held on the grounds. We stopped and disembarked the bus. When the crowd saw the band, it erupted. A banner hung between two trees, reading, 'Followers of Mellowtron Reunion'.

I recognized happy faces as we walked into the throng. The greasers were there, standing on the bumpers of their low riders and cheering. The crowd began to chant, "James Blank! James Blank! James Blank!" As much as crowds love to chant, I hadn't expected that one. I guess they were excited I wasn't deceased. Most of them already knew I wasn't dead, because I had been promoting the reunion on my internet radio station, but it felt good to be loved.

The mob swarmed us with hugs, pats on the back, tears of joy, and barbecue sandwiches. We had a picnic in the grass, then threw the Frisbee for a while, just like old times.

I looked at my watch and grew concerned regarding an

overdue arrival. As if on cue, an oversized diesel pickup pulling a flatbed trailer turned into the parking lot seconds before a panel truck did the same. I walked over to greet the drivers and arrange their synchronization. I directed the panel truck driver to back his rig up to the trailer.

I went back to the crowd now, which had become still. They were curious about what was happening.

"We need some volunteers," I said loudly. Two dozen hands raised.

"The gear in the back of that panel truck has got to be moved onto the flatbed trailer. The generators, too. Then we're going to do a quick soundcheck before we leave. We'll also need some people to ride on the trailer on the way to the gig to hold the equipment in place and make sure it doesn't fall off when we turn."

The crowd cheered, hopeful that they were about to see Mellowtron play live again, and rushed to action. The whole process took ten minutes.

The P.A. was wired up, powered by a quiet gas-fueled generator. Mike the Mike hooked up Cal's vocal microphone to let me speak to the crowd.

"   ," I said. The people yelled that they couldn't hear me. I turned to Mike, and he looked at the back of the P.A. with an irritated expression. His face relaxed when he saw the problem, and he looked at me and gave a thumbs-up.

"Can you hear me?" I asked, and reverberations of my voice bounced off the school and back to me. The crowd applauded.

"First of all, thank you for meeting us in beautiful Topeka, Kansas," I said. "I doubt most of you have been here before, but welcome, regardless." The crowd clapped, eager to hear what else I had to say.

"Secondly, I want to announce that you will see Mellowtron perform today!"

That's what they were waiting to hear. The announcement produced the loudest applause so far.

"I thought you'd like that," I said. "There's a few more surprises, as well. We have a new keyboard player. I'm happy to introduce Miss Cherry Topping!" I pointed at Cherry, and she smiled shyly and waved. Next, I caught Nicky's eye and mouthed, "Send the text." Nicky smiled and pressed the 'SEND' button on his phone.

A few seconds later, a vehicle pulled up behind me. It was the Loaves and Fishes van, which would soon be donated to the Hard Rock Casino in Vegas. The Loaves stumbled out, wearing their robes, and the crowd went bonkers. Most of them were original supporters of the Loaves, after all.

The crowd rushed toward the Loaves and Fishes, so I intervened. "Stop, everyone! Please go back to where you were. The Loaves won't be supplying the crowd like in the old days. They're famous rock stars now! You'll get to say 'hi' to them in a little while." The crowd murmured disappointment, but returned to where they stood before the band's surprise arrival.

Mellowtron and Nicky strolled over to greet the Loaves in the parking lot behind me. I hoped I could hold the people's attention.

"I know we're all excited," I said, "but can everyone please pay close attention now? It's vitally important."

The people hushed. I looked out across hundreds of earnest faces.

"Does anybody know where we are?" I asked.

"Topeka!" a man yelled.

"More specifically," I said.

"Monroe Elementary School in Topeka, Kansas!" a woman shouted.

"Yes," I said. "That's exactly right. Next question – does anyone know *why* we're here?"

Nobody spoke.

"We're here to make a stand and settle a score," I said. "That building behind you, Monroe Elementary School, was ground zero for the end of segregation in American schools. This is the place where the fight to end the separation of whites and blacks in education started!"

The crowd cheered, and I felt like a politician.

"Where would we be without that? Remember when we toured through the South with Mellowtron? We were accepted!"

The crowd exploded.

"Today, we are going to make a statement about love and acceptance in America, the finest country on earth. The country that has done more for oppressed peoples than any other in human history. The country that has sacrificed hundreds of thousands of its own sons to die protecting freedom around the globe. What other nation has done that? We fought and destroyed Nazi Germany. We defeated Imperial Japan. We kicked Fascist Italy's ass! We sent Soviet Russia back to their shinebox! Communist China doesn't wanna mess with us!" The crowd cheered, and a chant started. "U-S-A! U-S-A!"

I raised my hands to quiet them. "Yes, we can definitely kick ass, when necessary," I said. "But there's another way to communicate, and we Americans are great at that, too – through peace, love, and harmony. We're gonna spread a message of peace and love today, even if we have to kick a little ass to do it! Mellowtron is back!!"

The crowd clapped ecstatically and again chanted, "U-

S-A! U-S-A!"

I raised my hands again. "First, though, we need to do a very quick tune-up and soundcheck. Load up in your vehicles and get ready to follow us, just like you used to do. We're only traveling a short distance. When we finish playing, we'll head back to the school for a 'meet and greet'. After that, Mellowtron will be heading back to Alabama. Please don't follow. Keep listening to my internet radio station, and I'll make sure all of you are the first to know about Mellowtron's next tour. ALL ABOARD THE PEACE TRAIN!"

Mellowtron and the Loaves hurried to the flatbed, and the followers rushed to their vehicles. The soundcheck was performed post-haste, and the instruments were placed back in their cases and returned to the storage compartment of the old bus.

We drove extremely slow to keep the equipment from falling off the trailer when accelerating and turning. With the line of cars behind us, it was almost like a parade. Or a funeral procession. Eventually, we arrived at our destination – the Westside Baptist Church. I was surprised to see the perimeter was surrounded by an iron fence.

The truck pulled the flatbed stage to a spot directly in front of the building. The followers found parking places wherever they could. The church only has about forty members, so the streets weren't congested.

The Sunday morning service was taking place inside, so we tried to be as quiet as possible, both out of respect and to preserve the element of surprise. Skunk opened the hold of the bus for the band to retrieve the instruments, which were hustled to the flatbed and quickly plugged in. Everything was ready.

I whistled to catch everyone's attention. I extended my

index finger in the air and whipped it around like a tornado. The followers knew what that signal meant. They hurried to ring the entire perimeter of the church grounds and locked hands.

Without warning, Crisco barked excitedly at something in the hold of the tour bus, and Akeldama burst forth from the vehicle. Crisco was immediately on her heels in chase. The black dog jumped the high fence and galloped toward the church. She threw her wolf-sized body against the front doors and burst inside.

The Westside congregation shrieked in terror, as if a gunman had just walked through the doorway. More than likely, they were terrified of exactly that.

"Black Shuck has come for us!" the pastor wailed. The church members fled the building like it was on fire and then froze, seeing that they were surrounded.

Sponge clicked his sticks four times, and Headley played a lead on his guitar, which was an approximation of the horns normally heard at the beginning of the song, and we all sang three words – "Love, love, love."

Cal had no problem remembering the lyrics this time. He channeled John Lennon, singing 'All You Need Is Love'.

The followers joined in, hand in hand, and sang along – a 300 person choir. The Westside church members stood in shocked silence. I knew how they felt. It was similar to the awkward moment when you open your door and find a bunch of people belting out Christmas carols. That's what we were subjecting the Westside people to, on a somewhat grander scale. We wanted to send these 'Christians' a message of love they would never forget. At first, they looked furious and irritated, but that changed as a connection was made. Women cried openly, and men fought back tears, questioning how much hate had to do with religion.

The song ended, and nobody knew what to do next. I had been remiss in my planning. Domino stepped to his microphone and warbled, "I'd like to teach the world to sing in perfect harmony."

Those who recognized the line from the seventies television commercial laughed, then sang along. "I'd like to buy the world a Coke and keep it company."

The Loaves sang, "Love, love, love," and the two songs somehow intertwined, meshing into a glorious choral declaration of the sovereign American Spirit that went on for fifteen minutes. I looked out and saw people of every color and creed singing their hearts out in a glorious message of unity.

Several women who looked to be in their early twenties ran to the gate and out of the church's confines to join the followers. The young men stayed, more loyal to their religious obligation.

Finally, the singing stopped, and the Westside Church pastor yelled toward the musicians on the trailer, whom I had joined. He had a Bible in one hand and gestured at us with the other.

"How could you do this to us? Why did you send that devil-dog into our church service?"

"Why do you protest at the funerals of young Americans who gave their lives in service of our country?" I said into a microphone. With all that P.A. power behind me, I sounded like God compared to him.

"God hates fags! You are going to Hell! God hates all of you!" he screamed rabidly.

Mike the Mike cranked the P.A. up to eleven, and I commanded from my trailer on high, "THE ONLY THING GOD HATES IS HATE," which nearly knocked the pastor down. Everyone on our side cheered wildly.

"We leave you with a message of love," I said, my words echoing all over Topeka. "WE LOVE YOU ALL!!"

Everybody cheered again, even some of the Westside people. I stepped away from the microphone, and the followers walked back to their cars.

"Meet at the school," I yelled, and the word passed through the crowd.

Back at the original meeting spot, Mellowtron and the Loaves had a giant meet and greet and signed hundreds of autographs before treating the followers to an acoustic jam. It was just like old times.

That was the last we saw of Akeldama, thank God. We had no way of knowing it, but Akeldama was a demon who had walked the earth in many forms since the time of Judas Iscariot. Hell, she was there when Judas hanged himself. She knocked the stool right out from under him.

***

We had a happy trip back to Alabama, and the band was elated by a special surprise when we got home. I enlisted Roy Lee and his crew of redneck carpenters to complete the studio while we were gone. I had decided the boys had committed enough of themselves to the project, and it was time to concentrate solely on music.

Roy Lee's boys had also bulldozed the front yard, other than the trees lining the path. We'd be playing croquet and bocce in the near future. Eventually, I'd have the bowling alley repaired and updated by Roy Lee, as well. I decided to leave the broken fountain in the back as it was. A fire is much better to have a singalong around than a fountain, after all.

CHAPTER FIFTEEN

One day not long after we got back from Kansas, a knock came at the door while I was working on the computer. The boys were in the studio, as usual. I walked over and looked out the peephole and couldn't believe my eyes.

It was my dad – Coach. My hands began to quiver uncontrollably, and I felt like a four-year-old again. I opened the door, but couldn't speak.

"Is this where Lucy O'Day lives?" he asked. He didn't recognize me. "She's my mother."

"N-n-no," I said. Coach looked at me like I was an idiot.

"I coulda swore this was her house," he said. "But that was forty years ago. Man, you sure look familiar. Do I know you?"

"We've never met," I said. "I'm sorry, but I'm very busy. Good luck finding your mother."

I shut the door and looked out the peephole as my father walked away. I stumbled to the kitchen table and put my head in my hands, searching for understanding of what had just happened and what it meant.

Lucy O'Day was the name of the debutante I worked for. Coach said Lucy O'Day was his mother. That meant the old debutante was my grandmother. It all made perfect sense – in the most incoherent and random way.

But what about my name? I thought. *Shouldn't it be James O'Day?* I searched my mind, and another forgotten memory floated back.

***

It was the first day of kindergarten. Melba, the nice lady I had lived with for the last year after my mother's suicide, was enrolling me. She had a piece of paper listing the shots I had received.

"What's the boy's name?" the school secretary asked. There was a long line of kids and parents behind us.

"His name be James," my unofficial adoptive mother said.

"Yes, James what?" the lady asked as she filled out the enrollment card.

My new mother looked worried. She didn't know my last name.

"I'm not rightly sure his last name," she said.

The secretary looked exasperated and surveyed the long line behind us. "I can't just leave the box empty," she said. "I need a last name."

"Jus' leave it blank," my new mom said, not knowing what else to say.

The secretary wrote BLANK behind my first name on the enrollment form.

***

I raised my head from my hands and stared at the wall in front of me. *This was the last forgotten memory. My past was complete.*

I laughed, and Crisco hopped into the chair across the table from me and smiled.

"I guess both of us are just mutts," I said. "But we've got a lot of terrier in us. That's a good thing."

Crisco barked sharply two times and stared into my eyes like only a terrier will, communicating happiness.

"Let's go for a walk," I said. "We can't neglect our health regimen."

Crisco and I strolled to the mulberry tree, walking slowly. I searched in vain for arrowheads, hoping to find one to add to Cherry's collection.

When we reached the tree, I sat on the ground with my

back against it. Crisco laid down next to me and put his head on my thigh.

"I never thought I'd see Coach again," I said. "I never thought I'd see you, either." Crisco's eyes found mine, but he didn't say anything. "Now I know my real last name. I guess everything happens for a reason."

We fell asleep and woke as the sun was setting. I watched the colors mingle on the horizon until I got cold. Music drifted to me on the breeze.

"The guys are practicing," I said. "Sounds like a new song. We better get home."

***

We arrived at the house, and there was a fire burning in the entertainment lounge. It had been started in the fireplace on purpose, though – Akeldama was long gone. I stuck my head in the room, but nobody was there. Crisco walked over and laid down by the hearth to nap.

I went upstairs. I could hear activity in the recording studio as I passed level two. It sounded like they were mixing a new song. I kept going up to the third floor. I was confident the new track would be awesome – all the others were. I would hear it when it was done. I was giving up some of the control to Mike and the band, so as not to be too choleric. Robo taught me that.

I entered my radio broadcast studio and sat down in my driver's seat. I flipped numerous switches to the 'ON' position and turned on the laptop. There wasn't a proper light in the room. I relied on the electronics to provide ambient illumination. That's the way I wanted it.

The computer booted up, and the limiter and equalizer flickered to life. Tubes glowed through the vent holes in the back of the pre-amp and emulator. I pulled the microphone down to its place in front of my mouth. The digital clock flashed from from 9:59 to 10:00.

"It's that time again, my friends. Good evening from the Hotel Alabama. James Blank is back on the radio, and I come to you on gossamer wings transmitted. There's a full moon tonight, and I can see every star in the sky. I can see all of you, too. I see you in your bedrooms. You've got headphones on. I see you doing your homework. I see you playing video games. I see you reading 'Band On The Run'. And to all of you smoking weed, I promise not to tell your parents. I know you're all hanging on my every little word. There's thousands of you – thousands of *us*."

"Let's get right to it. The first tune of the evening is one of my absolute favorites." I cued 'You and I' by Queen, from the album 'A Day At The Races'. As the song played, I alternated between playing air drums and pantomiming the incredible vocals. I even pulled out my air guitar for the solo. Moments like this were why I had always wanted to be a deejay.

For effect, I waited fifteen seconds after the song ended, my airwaves dead air. I tapped the microphone with my fingers. "Okay. Is everyone ready? Is everybody in? We're going to experience something together this evening. I want you to turn off all the lights in your room. Open the window shades and look at the moon. If there's a tree or something in the way, and you can't see, crank up your speakers and climb out your window and lay down in the grass where you have a better view." I waited a minute while I let 'Somebody To Love' play very softly.

I used my wireless mouse to pull the fader on the music down to zero db before I spoke again. "As you can see, the moon is full tonight – it's as big as I've ever seen. There's a star to the right of it – the brightest star in my sky. You might find it a little up or down or to the left, depending on where you are, but it's the most brilliant star closest to the moon. I want you to find it and focus on it while I play the next song. Think about your life and my life – all our lives. We're connected in this universe." Just then a yellow meteor traced between the bright star and the moon.

"Wow!" I said. "Did you see that?"

All over the world, people said, "YES!"

"That is so cool," I said. "I knew tonight was going to be special. Let's all make a wish."

The shooting star wasn't part of my plan, and it threw me off for an instant, but I am a professional. Finding inspiration, I quickly located and cued a song on my laptop. The track I played was 'Atlantis' by Donovan. With its repeated refrain of 'way down below the ocean', it may seem odd that my inner muse had guided me to this choice, but enchanted serendipity had reared its beautiful head once again. An idea I had meditated on at the mulberry tree with Crisco was now born, fully formed and ready to be broadcast worldwide. Namely, the conception that the ocean and outer space are synonyms in the universe's thesaurus. They're both cold and lonely, and the pressure can be too much if you don't have a special helmet and suit.

As the song came to an end, it inspired the next one, as so often happens. James Blank, if I may refer to myself in the first person, took a left turn here and did something that will shock you to the core of your being. *I played a new song*. A new song that perfectly captured the moments in my immediate past – the last ten minutes, to be more clear. This is where I have some explaining to do – to you, the reader, but not to my listeners on that night. Luckily for them, they just heard what I played and had their minds blown out en route to nirvana. Sadly, I have to explain it to you, but I will not offer excuses. I played a *new* song about a falling star by

a *new* group called 'Florence + The Machine'.
***

I know you're contemplating shoving this book down the garbage disposal and cursing me as a traitor to British rock, but please hear me out. After my years in near comatose exile, I had hungrily sought out what was new in the world when the internet came into my life. I explored popular culture, Snooki and all. Suicide would have been my fate if I hadn't run across a precious handful of artists that restored my faith in humanity and the arts – Kid Cudi, Slaid Cleaves, Ryan Adams, Knaan, The Sword, Gentleman's Pistols, Band of Horses, Foxy Shazam, along with a few others. These discoveries informed me that music had not died while I was gone and aided my recovery and will to live, since they all contained and conveyed the vital human spirit to me when I needed it most. And isn't that what great music always does? I also, for the first time, explored albums like 'Get the Knack' and 'But Seriously, Folks' and found gems I had somehow missed the first time around. There was even an awesome new Van Halen album with Diamond Dave on vocals. Unbelievable.

So now 'Florence' has been justified, I guess – but not quite. I also must say that the Florence songs I came to love so much were YouTube live versions accompanied by not much more than harp and piano, which I ripped to mp3. When I listened to the album versions of these songs, I felt claustrophobic. There was so much needless bombast and over-production. I won't elaborate further, other than to reiterate that I played *live* versions of the songs – unplugged and achingly beautiful. Please seek them out if you want to re-create my playlist. (hint - AOL sessions)
***

The song about the falling star was called 'Cosmic

Love', and that's what we all felt as we stared at that bright star together. There was a transcendental connection being made across time and space.

Next, I played another live song by Florence, which completed my ocean/space metaphor. Somewhat out of character for my Wolfman Jack-style radio persona, I did not speak between the songs. I simply played a track called 'Never Let Me Go'. This tune's lyrics were from the perspective of being at the bottom of the ocean, looking up, which completed my poetic comparison. I had progressed from my early days, pretending to deejay from behind the wheel of the Sopwith Camel. Now my radio shows had specific themes, and I viewed them as something of an art.

As the song played softly, I was finally compelled to speak. I gave a voice-over like Carl Sagan narrating an episode of 'Cosmos', interjecting my thoughts between vital musical passages.

"Look up and think about the vastness of it all. It's like we're sitting at the bottom of an ocean, viewing the fractured light of the moon flickering on the surface miles above us. The sky is the ocean our minds swim in tonight. We've all been to the moon, and we've all been to the bottom of the sea – life's ups and downs. But *tonight* we are all exactly where we're supposed to be – under the same exact star. We're connected by the spirit of radio. Forever."

I cued the next song, and crisp notes from an acoustic guitar opened it – 'Across The Universe'. John Lennon's soothing voice assured me and my listeners that nothing was ever gonna change our world. Gazing up into vast infinity, it had a special meaning to everyone participating in this exercise. I knew thousands of people were hearing the song with me, meditating on the same star I was gazing out my window at. The song seemed to last forever, so languid and bittersweet.

As the song faded away, I spoke softly.

"And with that I bid you goodnight, for tomorrow I will travel. I hope you'll forgive me for this evening's short set. The new Sopwith Camel is gassed up, and the gear is loaded, ready to go on tour in the morning. If I meet you down the road somewhere, say to me, 'teo torriate', and I will stay a while. I got that from a Queen song, but you know that, don't you?"

"Until I see you again – my sky is wide open...."

I cued the last song on the Queen album I had played to start the set and clicked the 'REPEAT' button on the computer's media player. The record's final song, 'Teo Torriate', would play for the next three months, over and over and over and over. You'd laugh if you knew how many people listened to it night after night.

AUTHOR'S NOTE

I was listening to James' broadcast on my phone that night while I was driving to the Hotel Alabama. I was just outside Stringtown, and I pulled my car over to gaze into the heavens with him. It was one of the most magical experiences of my life. It felt like James was talking to me. He was, I guess – to me and thousands of others.

When I arrived at the Hotel Alabama, I was met with mixed feelings. Nicky tried to punch me, but James stopped him and told everyone I was not the enemy. I never tried to hurt any of them by doing 'Band On The Run', after all. I only published James' diary to document Mellowtron, one of the best bands ever. I never made a dime off it.

We worked things out, and I went on tour with Mellowtron again. I have been a resident of Hotel Alabama since we returned, holed up in a little room writing 'Running On Empty' using James' notes. The band has finished recording and is now mixing and mastering their new triple album, which will be self-released in a few weeks. It's the best stuff they've ever done. Cherry has added so much – she's playing the synthesizer like she's been taking lessons from John Paul Jones. The Loaves and Fishes are staying at the Hotel Alabama, guesting on the new Mellowtron album and recording their own, as well. It's a bit like a rock-n-roll fantasy camp at the moment. And it's a blast.

The new 'Tron album is called 'Astrophysical Graffiti'. Headley had a lot to do with the title, obviously, although he took one frustrating night of recording difficulties too seriously and unsuccessfully tried to throw the master tapes into the fire pit. The songs sound like a cross between the best Led Zeppelin and the best Pink Floyd. Crisco and Sponge have created the most essential kick drum sound in the history of rock and roll. Headley played his six-string with a cello bow on many of the songs, and it will re-define the electric guitar. Cal's voice is in fine form, and Domino is, well... Domino.

And Crisco's Facebook page has 900,000 'likes'.

www.ingramcontent.com/pod-product-compliance
Lightning Source LLC
Chambersburg PA
CBHW060154050426
42446CB00013B/2820